Praise for

MW01076209

"This book is a remarkable meditation on the deep loves of the heart, how these have difficulty finding a home within a misdirected imagination, and how they can alternatively express themselves fruitfully and faithfully. The Sweedens have given us a timely and fitting gift for our moment; those who feel restless or who seek to care for the restless will find here a pertinent, clarifying, edifying, and hortatory word."

Daniel Castelo, PhD
Duke Divinity School
Durham, NC

"Holiness in a Restless World is a wonderful read about pilgrimage, finding our home in God, laying down our heroic instincts, voluntarily displacing ourselves, and discovering how God is at work in us in normal, everyday practices. Nell and Josh have drawn deeply from Scripture, contemplative writers, and the words of John Wesley to weave together an engaging and important book for all who are serious about following Christ. It's time to settle in a comfortable spot, brew some tea, and listen to what God might be saying to you through these pages. I highly recommend this book."

Ron Benefiel, PhD
Point Loma Nazarene University
San Diego, CA

"How wonderfully fitting that spouses—who share everyday routines and moments—put their heads and hearts together to write *Holiness in a Restless World*, encouraging us to be open to holy encounters with God in the 'improvisation of daily life.' Rather than pursuing a heroic Christianity, which has had detrimental consequences, the Sweedens invite us into holiness as an ordinary, earthy endeavor, rooted in love of God and neighbor. For anyone who has ever felt restless or wayward—i.e., everyone—you'll find yourself wandering home through these pages."

Priscilla Pope-Levison, PhD
Perkins School of Theology
Dallas, TX

"Even if we aren't always aware of it, the frenetic pace of our lives in this busy age can quickly close off our capacity to see the beauty and goodness of everyday life. We can often be left wondering if the day-to-day has any meaning beyond itself, or if there is much joy to be found in the everyday. Taking seriously the pressures we face each day, *Holiness in a Restless World* offers a deep well of time-honored resources that may surprise you with their capacity to open life to a joyful movement of wonder, love, and praise."

Timothy R. Gaines, PhD
Trevecca Nazarene University
Nashville, TN

"Nell and Josh have provided new whimsical metaphors for helping us understand that the holy life is both a home to be found and a journey to be walked in wonder. The narrative role of a theologian is to take the grand truths of Scripture and historical doctrines, and translate them in such a way that they are understood in new contexts and new eras. This book is a much-needed resource in that translation task, bringing fresh insight to the experiential realities of holiness and sanctification today."

Diane Leclerc, PhD
Northwest Nazarene University
Nampa, ID

"Coalescing the biblical notion of home with the theme of holiness, the Sweedens help us recapture the value of ordinary practices in Christian life that are essentially communal in nature and serve as a responsible corrective to variegated forms of individualistic heroism lodged in our contemporary context. *Holiness in a Restless World* is insightful, reflective, and powerfully generative; it is a must-read for all who take seriously the task of Christians to respond with discernment to the questions of many who remain restless today."

David Sang-Ehil Han, PhD
Pentecostal Theological Seminary
Cleveland, TN

HOLINESS

in a

RESTLESS

WORLD

JOSHUA R. SWEEDEN
NELL M. BECKER SWEEDEN

THE FOUNDRY
PUBLISHING

Copyright © 2022 by Joshua R. Sweeden and Nell M. Becker Sweeden
The Foundry Publishing®
PO Box 419527
Kansas City, MO 64141
thefoundrypublishing.com

978-0-8341-4156-8

Printed in the
United States of America

Cover design: Brandon Hill
Interior design: Sharon Page

Library of Congress Cataloging-in-Publication Data
A complete catalog record for this book is available from the Library of Congress.

The internet addresses, email addresses, and phone numbers in this book are accurate at the time of publication. They are provided as a resource. The Foundry Publishing does not endorse them or vouch for their content or permanence.

10 9 8 7 6 5 4 3 2 1

For Eli and Asher
May you continue to be bearers of the beauty of the gospel

Instructions for living a life:
Pay attention.
Be astonished.
Tell about it.
—Mary Oliver, excerpted from "Sometimes"

ᴄᴏCONTENTS

WANDERING HOME

Home is an ever-present theme in Christian Scripture—not a nostalgic or romanticized vision of home but a home centered around peace, promise, and belonging. Much of Scripture tells of a type of homelessness—being cast out, sent forth, exiled, or stripped of land. Occasionally, God's people are "at home" even as they reside in foreign lands, living in the liminal spaces and margins somewhere between their past and promised future. God's people do a lot of wandering, which only enhances and reiterates the narrative of home in Scripture. Wandering is not the absence of home, but it represents the temporality, transience, and insecurity that can occur when we do not feel at home, and so remains a testimony to the theological significance of home and the ultimate importance of God's people finding peace and belonging with God and in the world. While alienation from home is sometimes construed as a type of punishment for unfaithfulness, equally common are the images of a God who makes a home and dwells among his people. When it comes to God and God's people, home matters.

The parable of the prodigal son in Luke 15:11–32 offers one of the most decisive and recognizable narratives of home in Christian Scripture. Like a microcosm of the narrative arc of Scripture, the parable gives as much attention to the son's separation from home—his own restlessness and sense of urgency in establishing self-identity—as it does to descriptions of home itself. The clearest characteristic of home, besides the apparent prosperity and security afforded by this household, is the familial bond represented in both the misguided love of the older brother and the unconditional love of the father. The latter, of course, represents the nature and character of God. At the climactic point when the father embraces the lost and wandering son, the meaning of the parable is clear: home is in and with God. The son is lost—without familial identity and lacking heirship—until the parental, all-encompassing embrace restores the son to the peace, promise, and belonging that only comes with participation in the household of God.

This book is about wandering and belonging, restlessness and peace. It is written for wanderers attempting to make their way home through all the snares, distractions, and fleeting visions of peace and belonging that compete for our attention. The Christian life is a journey juxtaposed by a destination—a home, a place. The journey finds its meaning through the promise of belonging and participation in the household of God. But what if the wanderer loses sight of the house? It can be easy to wander in vain. There are enough false and mistaken destinations to fill many lifetimes. Although a journey may warrant or benefit from detours, endless wandering without trajectory or purpose may eventually lead to nihilism. If the parable of the prodigal son is at all analogous to the Christian journey—God's call, our grace-empowered move toward God, and God's full-fledged embrace of us—then the purpose of this book is to help Christians distinguish between the mirages and the true promised land.

More specifically, this book is written for Christians who have been taken captive by the restlessness of our age—prodigals themselves who have taken the path of the misguided hero, pursuing rest in the wrong places: achievement, importance, approval. Such heroes are never satisfied and never fulfilled. They are always chasing, always consuming, always frantic. Like the adventure junkie dependent on the next rush of adrenaline, the misguided hero is afraid to slow down and let go of a perceived sense of control. To rest, we must face our demons, instead of conquering the next mountain that serves as both a welcome distraction and an opportunity to earn admiration. The church is entwined with our restless world and has shared in the idealization and idolization of the hero. This error has stalled and stunted the story's arc, leaving the prodigal child plagued by endless wandering toward fleeting fulfillment. The story's culmination and the full embrace of God remains, maybe more so than ever, only a reflection, as in a mirror (1 Cor. 13:12).

The following chapters are expansions of lectures we first offered in the spring of 2019 as the Hicks Holiness Lectures at Mount Vernon Nazarene University. Those lectures, directed toward an undergraduate audience, intended to offer an alternative vision of Christian faithfulness to the commonly elevated narratives of heroic and extraordinary Christianity. Such narratives offer a misconstrued vision of holiness that neglects the primary, more general, and sometimes more difficult task of living faithfully in the ordinary and everyday matters of life. Savior mentality runs rampant in contemporary evangelicalism and for various reasons has also found a strange resonance within the Wesleyan-Holiness tradition. Our aim is to counter this mentality with a message that is timely and applicable to all Christians no matter their life experience or faith development.

Poetry can offer insight and perspective where prose fails, and we have learned that the oft-concealed theological imagination of a Wendell Berry or Mary Oliver may be exactly what our contemporary world needs to encounter. Our earlier lectures followed a recitation of the opening stanza of the poem "Allegiances," by William Stafford. Like Berry and Oliver, Stafford is a poet and essayist who employs overtones of land, community, and commonplace to speak to (or against) our modern selves. The chapters of this book draw from Stafford's opening lines:

> *It is time for all the heroes to go home*
> *if they have any, time for all of us common ones*
> *to locate ourselves by the real things*
> *we live by.*[1]

The connection between our thesis and Stafford's opening stanza will become increasingly evident with each chapter. Little needs to be expounded here, save for the underlying theme that the empty promises of heroism are exposed by the common, real, and placed things of life. Heroes lack a home—a place and community. The absence of home is the absence of rest and peace. From a Christian perspective, the absence of home disconnects a person from true purpose and identity as one who belongs to and with God. In contrast to the heroic impulse, it is time for Christians to recover what it means to be placed in the commonwealth of God—to locate ourselves faithfully in the

---

1. William Stafford, "Allegiances," *Allegiances* (New York: Harper and Row, 1970), 77.

daily interactions and transactions of life with God's creation. Stafford does not write for a specifically Christian audience, nor is his project explicitly framed by a concern for greater theological understanding or embodiment of holiness. Yet his stanza is a succinct, far-reaching reminder of the limits of our commonly commodified version of holiness that idealizes heroism.

Holiness is characterized in two ways throughout this text. First, holiness is the pursuit of rest with God. This description is developed more fully in chapter 1 in connection with Augustine's adage that "our hearts are restless until they find their rest in thee." Pursuing—as much as being or arriving at—home with God remains central to the experience and embodiment of rest.

Second, holiness is encountered in the choreography of the quotidian. This characterization of holiness as an aspect of everyday life is an underlying theme of this book and rests on two assumptions. Foremost, holiness is an *encounter*. Holiness is sometimes misconstrued as something earned, achieved, or rewarded. But it is more properly a surprise, an experience, or even a confrontation with the beauty of God that is made evident through the effervescent work of the Spirit. Holiness is not a human work but the activity of a *wholly other* God who, in love, comes to and alongside creation. Like travelers on the road to Emmaus (Luke 24), holiness breaks in to our lives in unexpected ways, illuminating God and putting the reconciliation of all things on full display (Rom. 5:10–11; 2 Cor. 5:18–19). Understanding holiness as an encounter does not diminish the call to pursue holiness or to be holy as God is holy, but it does suggest that to pursue holiness is to have a posture of openness, having eyes to see and ears to hear (Mark 8:18). Additionally, holiness is an encounter that occurs in the improvisation of daily life. Scripture testifies to a God made known most commonly and consistently in simple and ordinary ways. God comes to us in our humanity. In the case of the Emmaus travelers, their eyes were opened after "he took bread, blessed and broke it, and gave it to them" (Luke 24:30). Daily living, like the Christian journey, is anything but a linear path or clear-cut road. As humans, we engage in a choreography—a dance—with other persons and with all God's creation. In the creativity, responsiveness, imagination, and even missteps of the dance, we encounter holiness. The beauty of God finds us in such moments in surprising and unexpected ways. Even still, the call to pursue holiness is not relinquished. We do not passively wait on God but strive for God's kingdom and righteousness (Matt. 6:33). On occasion, we may even surprise ourselves as, by God's grace, we are empowered to do justice, love kindness, and walk humbly with God (Micah 6:8).

In several ways (not every way), the titular character and protagonist of Wendell Berry's heralded novel *Jayber Crow* is an expression of the holiness journey. Jayber Crow is not the hero readers expect. In many ways, he is an antihero. As a young man, he leaves his community and his perceived calling in search of meaning and personal identity. He is driven by typical notions of heroism—significance, exotic experiences—but his journey away actually takes him home to Port William, Kentucky. There he finds himself and his true purpose in the simple and ordinary rhythms of community life. His path meanders. He becomes the town barber, the church custodian, and the city's gravedigger. In most ways, his life is mundane and uneventful, yet he is the embodiment of love for his neighbor and community. He enriches the lives of those around him as he works for the harmony and preservation of his community. By the end of the book, readers cannot help but be captivated by the peace and power that come with belonging. Jayber Crow is home and knows who he is. For Christians, such belonging includes place, people, and connection with God. There is peace and power on the other side of misguided heroism. Jayber's openness to being shaped by the Port William community and its needs—to going where called and filling the voids in everyday life—symbolizes a type of Christian pilgrimage. Jayber's journey is not bound by a destination or a prescribed arrival. Instead, it is the accumulation of little moments, twists and turns, many unexpected.

John Muir, the American naturalist and evangelist for the revealed beauty of God in creation, is known to have disliked the word "hike" and its connotation with a linear path and specified destination. Albert Palmer, traveling with Muir in the Sierra Nevada, once asked:

"Mr. Muir, someone told me you did not approve of the word 'hike.' Is that so?" Muir replied, "I don't like either the word or the thing. People ought to saunter in the mountains—not 'hike!' Do you know the origin of that word saunter? It's a beautiful word. Away back in the middle ages people used to go on pilgrimages to the Holy Land, and when people in the villages through which they passed asked where they were going, they would reply, *A la sainte terre*, 'To the Holy Land.' And so they became known as sainte-terrers or saunterers. Now these mountains are our Holy Land, and we ought to saunter through them reverently, not 'hike' through them."[2]

Whether in the mountains or not, pilgrims in the holy life must learn to saunter.

2. John Muir, *Spiritual Writings: Selected with an Introduction by Tim Flinders* (Maryknoll, New York: Orbis Books, 2013), 106.

PART I

Not All Who Wander Are Lost

It is time for all the heroes to go home
if they have any, time for all of us common ones
to locate ourselves . . .[1]

---

1. Stafford, "Allegiances."

It is time—time to imagine a world and the Christian life beyond the narratives and frameworks that have been fashioned by modern, Western paradigms. It is time to dismantle the hero within ourselves who owes its prototype and ideal not to the gospel but to our own restlessness. This, of course, is no easy task. We are captive to our contexts and the formation and perspectives that have taught us how to see and engage the world. But new imagination requires introspection and a willingness to be self-critical. In this sense, it must come from within, from a yearning for change.

The first part of this book acknowledges that we are lost, though not without hope. Being lost is different from wandering or meandering. Lost is a condition of missing identity, like forgetting who and whose we are and abandoning our *place* in the world. Wandering or meandering, on the other hand, are components of a journey. Sometimes that journey may be contra-directional, but it is nonetheless still formational and informative. God invites us on a journey, and the first step of that journey is to dislodge ourselves from any distorted visions of Christian life and formation that undermine the Christlike character we are to pursue.

Established Christianity in the Western hemisphere is facing an identity crisis. Such statements seem increasingly ubiquitous as churches experience declining membership and attendance or mourn their waning cultural and societal influence. It is appropriate to lament loss, especially because much of it remains ambiguous. There is no clear personage to blame, no decisive moment, no irrefutable logic that can explain the church's loss of social and cultural status. Of course, that hasn't stopped persons from trying to override ambiguity with certainty. Yet God's unfolding work cannot be envisioned if God's people simply long to return to Egypt (see Exod. 14:10–12; 16:3;

Neh. 9:17). Nor can it be encountered if, in our arrogance, we try to forge our own path and establish our own promised land. There is a balance in the Israelite exodus story from Egypt. Though they wander in the wilderness, uncertain of their future, they are also guided by the pillar of cloud by day and the pillar of fire by night (Exod. 13). Their journey is not aimless. God never leaves them even though their impatience and idolatry must be confronted and their trust in God repeatedly renewed.

The identity crisis of established Christianity in the West is deeper than the symptoms of institutional or cultural loss. It demands laying bare or uncovering the assumptions that have guided Christian practice so that we may sift through the pressing narratives and formations of our contemporary lives. Part I attends to the prevalence of heroic narratives in Christianity and calls attention to their influence on modern expressions of holiness. Heroism, of course, is but one idol, one mirage, in our journey with God. Yet it is particularly potent, especially in the way it exchanges trust and peace with God for constant restlessness.

one

OUR HEARTS ARE RESTLESS

Augustine of Hippo, a fourth-century theologian, famously wrote, "Our hearts are restless until they find their rest in thee." Holiness is the pursuit of a heart at rest—not a dormant, inactive, or idle heart but a heart properly oriented toward God; a heart at peace that *rests* in the full assurance of God's faithfulness and reconciling power. A heart at rest is a free heart. It is free *from* the distorted desires that define our world (influence, material gain, social approval) and free *for* an ever-deepening life in Christ for the sake of the world. A free heart is not an empty or autonomous heart, and it is not a heart that is absent of relationship or responsibility. That is a modern and narrow version of freedom. Instead, a free heart is full of right affection toward God and neighbor that is bound by relationship and constantly moved toward action.

A heart at rest translates to a life on the move. Yet the movement of the holy life is different from the frantic, directionless movement of a restless world. It is not the busybodies about whom the apostle Paul warns in 2 Thessalonians 3, nor is it constant movement in pursuit of a world after our own image as we satisfy our personal need to save and be seen as saving. A heart at rest moves in the way of Jesus, which is squarely defined in the Christian tradition as *kenosis*: the act of self-emptying (Phil. 2:6). A holy heart has its home in God and is able to resist the common temptation to make its home in the world by being a physical, spiritual, or political savior.

Jesus himself faced these temptations. As Matthew 4 notes, Jesus was driven by the Spirit into the wilderness, where the tempter came to him—first tempting him to turn stones into bread, then to throw himself off the pinnacle of the temple so the angels would carry him, and finally to bow down to the tempter in exchange for all the kingdoms and splendors of the world. The temptations correspond with Jesus's messianic calling as savior of the social, religious, and political world: Feed the hungry! Demonstrate your divinity! Exert your dominion! In a single moment, the messianic mission could have been fulfilled. A restless heart could not have resisted such temptation because a restless heart has no peace, no home. But Jesus responded as one whose heart is truly free and full of right affection toward God. Rather than turning stones to bread Jesus cited the scripture, "one does not live on bread alone, but by every word that comes from the mouth of God" (Matt. 4:4; Deut. 8:3). Rather than leaping from the pinnacle of the temple for all to see, Jesus cited the scripture, "Do not put the Lord your God to the test" (Matt. 4:7; Deut. 6:16). Rather than bowing to Satan, Jesus cited Scripture a third time: "Worship the Lord your God, and serve only him" (Matt. 4:10;

see Deut. 10:20). Though subtle at first, there is a clear theme in the passage. Jesus subverts the temptation to save the world *by the terms of the world* as he responds to the tempter by reemphasizing his relationship with God. Jesus responds as one whose heart is at rest in the power and provision of God—as though a Son in God's home. The call to holiness is the call to pursue such rest, to become children of God's household.

Yet our world promotes restlessness with variant and competing desires that each seek to tempt and lure and together shape us into a constant state of what one theologian called "cosmopolitan homelessness."[1] This kind of transience—billed as freedom—only increases the likelihood of our individual and communal exploitation. A fickle and displaced heart is the easiest kind of heart to manipulate, and our societal, economic, and political systems are astute at using our impulses and insecurities to meet their ends while ensuring our wandering affections never find peace.

There may be no better symbol of our restless reality than our all-pervasive culture of consumerism. Consumerism is *built* on restlessness—specifically the restlessness of desire. It seeks to exploit that restlessness by ensuring the consumer is never satisfied, never content, never at peace. Products become obsolete by design. If planned obsolescence is not built into the product itself (a cell phone whose operating system is so outdated as to be virtually unusable within a few years), then perceived obsolescence is (new features and styles that make previous iterations of

---

1. John Howard Yoder, "See How They Go with Their Face to the Sun," *For the Nations: Essays Evangelical and Public* (Eugene, OR: Wipf and Stock, 2002), 51.

the same product seem old-fashioned and stale). Consumerism is also driven by the creation of desire, which is an incredibly scientific enterprise, as anyone in marketing knows. The industry of creating, satisfying, and manipulating desire produces a powerful cycle that feeds more than an economic system. It shapes our worldview and our interactions with others—including God. It also distorts our vision of the holy life.

Love of Heroes

Heroes, and our love for them, are an enduring symbol of human restlessness. The hero, and the narrative in which the hero is cast, can easily reflect and even nourish our misdirected desires if not weighed against the self-emptying way of Jesus. This recognition is especially important in our contemporary context, which merges paradigms of modernity and Western culture, making the heroic lens both pervasive and enticing. The concern here is not with heroes or heroism, per se, but with the uncritical adoption of a heroic lens, especially if that lens nurtures affections and dispositions that are contrary to the affections and dispositions of a heart at rest in God.

Heroes have long served an important role in the social construction of culture. Stories of heroes' perseverance and triumph instill and reassert values; their lives are examples, even if flawed, that inspire and shape generations. Christianity also relies on heroes to model Christian virtue and practice. From biblical heroes to ancient, medieval, and modern accounts of saints, martyrs, and missionaries, Christianity shows a strong tendency to celebrate the heroic. Even the Gospel stories are not free from the overlay of a heroic lens. Consider Gustaf Aulén's development of the *Christus Victor* atonement theory, which reflects heroic prose, borrowing triumphal military images from Rome and demonstrating the pervasive influence of Greek mythology on Western thought, including patristic Christian theology.[2]

Fictional heroes display extraordinary humanity, and their factual historic equivalents are understandably rare. The stories of such heroes have complexity and power that are shaped by context, elevated by circumstance, and reified by continued significance. In this sense, they cannot be replicated but serve an aspirational purpose. They are persons of legacy and legend, testimonies to human potential when "used by God." In this sense, it is entirely appropriate that biblical interpreters have applied the title "heroes of the faith" to Hebrews 11. Hero is an apt description so long as we read Hebrews 11 alongside Hebrews 12. In doing so, we are reminded that the faith of our ancestors was, by itself, incomplete. Hebrews 12:2 identifies Jesus as "the pioneer and perfecter of our faith." The exemplars of Hebrews 11 are "so great a cloud of witnesses" (12:1), models for our own journey but not heroes in the modern, self-reliant, individualized sense.

While heroes can play a vital role in the formation of Christian virtue and practice, it must also be acknowledged that Christianity's love of the heroic often extends too far. The heroic lens now permeates notions of Christian faithfulness and has established the idealization of the extraordinary. Many Christians believe they must *be* something more and *do* something more; they must stand apart and above in some way to demonstrate

---

2. See Gustaf Aulén, *Christus Victor: An Historical Study of the Three Main Types of the Idea of Atonement.*

their faithfulness. Undoubtedly, conversion implies change—the Christian life includes *something more*—but that should not be equated with heroic narratives or grand gestures. In fact, conversion foremost requires the transformation of our *ordinary* loves and habits. Popular culture contributes to the elevation of the extraordinary. Books, TV shows, news stories, and movies all testify to society's obsession with heroes. By and large, Christianity has found consonance rather than dissonance with society's elevation of the heroic.

The Lure of the Extraordinary

When I (Josh) was in junior high, my church youth group was holding a fundraiser by selling t-shirts with Christian sayings and images on them. I recall one t-shirt with an image of Jesus and bold words stating, "One Man CAN Change the World!" I remember being moved by the t-shirt's slogan and its implicit message. While Jesus was the *subject* of the shirt's image, I was its *object*. The slogan was actually for me. It said, *You can be special and extraordinary. You can do great things. Like Jesus, God wants you to change the world!* At this point you might see how, in my young mind, God was something like an image of Uncle Sam saying, "I Want YOU!"

Though harmless in many ways, this memory remains emblematic of much of my earliest understandings of Christian holiness. The stories told, and the exemplars most embraced, often reflected a common narrative strangely consistent with a John-Wayne-like rugged individualism. I remember feeling inadequate as a Christian due to my lack of extraordinariness. Such overt misunderstandings of holiness are, of course, relatively easy to identify and dispel. What we should find disconcerting is that underneath each explicit employment of a heroic lens lurks an implicit framework or worldview with great power to define and determine a vision of Christian faith.

Clergy and laypersons alike experience the pressure to be extraordinary. While few Christians would go so far as to argue that human salvation is dependent upon *extraordinariness*, the dangerous assumption that eternal, or heavenly, rewards are assigned according to the significance of one's earthly life is still common in Christianity. The assumption here is that God grants the great women and men of history extra reward. There is, of course, within Christian tradition a privileging of extraordinary saints, and to be considered among them has appeal. Stronger yet is the way notions of personhood and community have become captivated by the pretense of extraordinariness. More than ever it seems we are obsessed with what makes us unique and special, our identity being rooted in our individuality rather than the communities and traditions in which we participate.

Contemporary critiques of late-twentieth-century church models provide an interesting example. Despite being quick to name the dangers and flaws of attractional models of church growth, numerical calculations of success, and the church's overt pursuit of distinction, influence, and profile that is common in modern Christendom, some of the contemporary models of ministry success reflect the same elevation of the extraordinary—the same concern to stand out. In this regard, the metrics of a successful or ideal ministry only changed on a surface level. The influence and success of a minister or community that was once measured by church attendance, building size, or political significance is now being measured by online following, number of impressions, and how much influence a minister or community consistently generates. It appears the modern church's edifice complex has been replaced by a social-approval complex (social approval indicators are employed by social media platforms to drive engagement). This shift is to be expected considering the stories we tell and the ministry models and exemplars we most embrace. While exemplars of faithfulness are needed, and should certainly be celebrated, the implicit and often dangerous elevation of the heroic suggests that ordinary lives and activities bear little significance in comparison to extraordinary acts of extraordinary persons. It hardly needs to be said that such a distinction couldn't be further from the good news Jesus continually offers in the Gospels. Whether it is Jesus's honoring of the widow who gave her last two coins (Mark 12:41–44), or his blessing of the children (Matt. 19:14–15), or his intentional, repeated, and countercultural engagement with tax collectors, prostitutes, the sick, and the dispossessed, Jesus summarizes it himself, frequently saying the first will be last, and the last will be first (see Matt. 19:30). The kingdom of God is upside down. We might wonder, then, what place the paradigms of heroism and extraordinariness have in the household of God.

An Embedded Worldview

We should find it interesting that the iconic superheroes in pop culture live in a state of constant restlessness. Consider the superheroes that comprise the DC and Marvel universes. In most cases, they are emotionally unstable, relationally isolated, and struggling to regain any true sense of home. To their credit, many of them have endured immeasurable loss and, though they have supernatural abilities, struggle the most to make sense of seemingly natural and ordinary things, like love and friendship. These superheroes' weaknesses, not their strengths, are what make them so compelling.

There is an age-old formula to the story of a superhero. The superhero must have a relatable element. They must, in some way, reflect *us*—full of capacity, possibility, and flaws all at once. Their supernatural abilities are just that: *natural* abilities that have some-how been "super-sized." And there is just enough there for us to connect with the superhero, to empathize. Once that connection is made, the power of the story takes over. We envision being like the superhero, living hypothetically in their shoes.

I recall when my eldest son declared he wanted to be Batman for Halloween. I didn't even know he was aware of Batman, but I soon found out he was familiar with a whole range of superheroes I had never heard of. Prior to that point, he had always been a dinosaur, and when you asked him what he wanted to be, even with his early kindergarten vocabulary he spilled out, "paleontologist." Now, in first grade, he was making a shift. The world of superheroes had captivated him. It was as evident in his play as it was in his desire to be Batman for Halloween. I started noticing in his play that there was always competition going on. Someone needed saving, someone had been captured, someone needed to escape. Some triumph had to happen, some force of good was opposing evil, and somebody with some extraordinary ability always prevailed.

Naturally, my son was always the protagonist in his own stories. What hit me, though, was how quickly the heroic lens took hold and encapsulated almost all of his play. Fewer were the days when he would build a pillow fort just to build a fort or push a train or car just to "drive" them. It no longer satisfied him to mimic ordinary life; there had to be an element of the extraordinary. The pillow fort became a military base. The car had to be escaping some pending disaster or villainous person. Ordinary life now seemed insufficient to hold his attention. The impact of the heroic lens on understandings of Christian holiness is not dissimilar. Stories of heroism are powerful and transformative, and they satisfy, at least temporarily, some of the deep longings of our hearts: the need to be loved, to be noticed, to be important, to be valued. It is one thing for children to latch on to the stories of superheroes and integrate them into their play, but for many adults, the heroic lens is an escape. Like the prodigal son who leaves his home with visions of extraordinary experiences and in search of another self, the heroic lens can dangerously feed our wandering desires.

Heroism and Holiness

The intent of this chapter is not to criticize heroes or heroism. Heroes and their stories have an important function and can, if engaged properly, be fruitful for the development of Christian virtue and practice. The danger is when heroism becomes the lens for the Christian life—or, worse, when we begin to equate heroism with holiness. Heroism and holiness may have some compatibility, but they are undeniably distinct in that holiness is the pursuit of rest in God and heroism the outflow of restlessness.

Three patterns are generally evident when heroism becomes the lens of the Christian life and is equated with holiness. First, Christians struggle to celebrate the small things. What a hero sees is generally tainted by some pending doom or problem to be overcome. This lens disables the hero's ability to recognize the goodness of God's creation and celebrate beauty in the midst of tragedy. Similarly, holiness is narrowly identified with rare and exceptional things. The heroic lens privileges the newsworthy and attention-grabbing acts of our world, losing a vision of holiness as encompassing all of life—a vision that values the ordinary alongside the extraordinary. When Christians struggle to celebrate the small things, we ultimately struggle to recognize and receive the gifts of God and others. Heroes miss the simple gifts since an epic horizon is always the dominating view. But Christians are called to receive and respond to the gifts of God, which come to us daily in simple yet profound ways. Holiness entails an ever-deepening recognition of the gifts we receive and the ways we can, in turn, become gifts for others.

Second, when heroism becomes the lens of the Christian life and is equated with holiness, Christians fail to trust and depend on God. Lack of trust leads to insecurity, and insecurity breeds anxiety and defensiveness. Not surprisingly, the heroic lens supports a world of conflict and competition. In such a world, binaries are reinforced and established: right or wrong, good or bad, black or white. Christians become forced to adopt a posture of defense, inclined to judge people, cultures, communities, or ideas as for or against us. In a similar way, narratives of heroism predispose us to expect grand gestures and dramatic escapes. We look for and value the dramatic and then overlay those expectations onto our conception of God, the church, and others. Such misguided expectations not only set us up to be frustrated and discouraged, but they also invert the relationship between Creator and creation. Our expectations now set the rules for God's engagement with creation. And true to form, we quickly make ourselves the hero of the story: "One man *can* change the world—me!"

Trust in God, on the other hand, spurs faith in God as the Sustainer and Redeemer of the world. Holiness corresponds with assurance (security), not lack of confidence (insecurity). Assurance cultivates the fruit of the Spirit (Gal. 5:22–23), not anxiety and defensiveness. The notion that *we* have to save the world and that *we* have to usher in the kingdom reflects the heroic temptation. Much like Jesus in Matthew 3, our posture should instead be to reflect and point to God, the one who saves, conquers, heals, and redeems.

Third, when heroism becomes the lens of the Christian life, we confuse others' needs with our own need for self-worth. There are many examples of this confusion in Scripture, but few are as obvious as that of Jonah, who—after finally going to Nineveh to proclaim God's judgment—becomes angry with God for showing compassion to the Ninevites. What cause does Jonah have to be angry? Should God not be gracious and abounding in love? Jonah's anger is driven out of his own self-righteous indignation and a misconstrued sense of justice that revolves around his own perspective and self-interest rather than around God's desires for others. Such self-centeredness, taking the various forms of egotism, selfishness, and narcissism, is common in heroic narratives. But—much like Achilles, who makes the conscious decision to commit his own life and the lives those around him for the sake of personal fame—self-centered heroes are supposed to be warnings for us, not role models. When our love for heroes displaces or outweighs our love for God and neighbor, it becomes difficult to see past ourselves. The same misdirected affections that prioritize triumph prompt heroes to view themselves as God's archetypal agents in an epic storyline. Inevitably, even if accidentally, our love turns inward, and the story becomes about us rather than about God. Like Jonah, we lose sight of God's redemptive purposes, and we struggle to accept an outcome that doesn't satisfy our own need to win in what we believe is a story of heroes and villains.

The Christian tradition employs the language of idolatry in instances when we prioritize ourselves and our desires over God and God's desires. When our love turns inward, we are in danger of becoming idols unto ourselves. Holiness requires that we keep our gaze ever upon Jesus Christ, the founder and perfecter of our faith. The way of Christ is found in self-emptying, cruciform love. As long as our affections remain distorted, the way of Christ doesn't have quite the same allure as our own reflections in the water. Yet self-emptying, cruciform love is how we find our home in God. It is how our restless hearts truly find rest.

two

FINDING OUR REST IN GOD

When we return to the opening stanza of Stafford's "Allegiances," we find a conditional phrase after the heroes are sent home that is subtle and can be easy to miss. This phrase poses a much larger critique than first meets the eye. The phrase "if they have any" raises the question of why heroes might not have homes. Where did they come from? Where do they belong? The phrase is an especially potent critique of modernity and its tendency to value the universal over the particular. Heroes, of course, do have origins and homes, some more troubled and uncertain than others. Their origins compose an important part of their story. Who are Spider-Man, Batman, and Superman without Peter Parker, Bruce Wayne, and Clark Kent? Yet their particularity—their true personhood and identity as known by those who love them—is rarely celebrated. We give our attention to their heroic acts and accomplishments, as though their value is not in who they are but only in what they overcome, accomplish, or conquer. If heroes have a home, we have taken it from them by considering it unremarkable or inconsequential. Nobody wants a hero who goes home. We prefer a hero who rises above the commonplace and escapes the confines of daily life. A hero—especially a modern hero—is above (greater than) the particular. They are universal beings who fit our modern obsession with universal solutions; they reflect our own restlessness.

Truth be told, heroes do not appear from nowhere. They have been formed and shaped by a people and a place. They belong to a community, even if that community has rejected them. They have met challenges, learned from successes and failures, and have been influenced by others. Heroes journey and grow and come from *somewhere.* Our picture of the universal hero remains detached and disconnected from the formative contexts and communities in which all persons are enmeshed. Stafford reminds us that such heroes are aimless, if not ultimately destructive. They lack purpose and meaning, and they forever struggle to find their bearings. It is time for the universal hero to rediscover home, if they can. Time to return to rootedness, to that which centers.

Contemporary Christians must embark on a process of recalibration beyond the stories, privileging, and pressures of the universal hero. Recalibration requires unlearning false narratives and practices and disarming the individualistic tendencies that are inherent in the Western self. Christian formation foremost attends to the story of God through the lens of Jesus and the witness of the Spirit. Modern heroism presents a counter-story that is at once incredibly attractive and deceptive. While the hero escapes home, Christians should deepen our connection to home, seeking to live a holy life that is only possible by belonging to and finding rest in God.

Rediscovering home demands a journey that is both inward and outward. This chapter is devoted to the work of inward migration through the recovery of the particular, the significance of cultivation, and John Wesley's description of new birth. Subsequent chapters address the complementary work of outward movement.

The Scandal of Particularity

God's salvation and restoration of the world ironically involves few hero-like characters. Though we gravitate toward the special and extraordinary, Scripture largely emphasizes redemption through rather small and ordinary ways. God's work is universal in scope and purpose. All creation is redeemed. Yet it is worth acknowledging that God chooses to change the world by starting anew, at a particular point in history, with a single individual.[1] Appropriately we name Jesus, but before we jump to the manger in Bethlehem when the God-man entered the world, we must acknowledge that the plan to save the world began long before Jesus came to earth, with the faithfulness of Abram, "a wandering Aramean" (Deut. 26:5). German theologian Gerhard Lohfink exposes this underlying biblical theme. After the unraveling of God's intentions, the expansion of humanity, the universal impact of the flood, and even the universalizing intent of the Tower of Babel, God began a plan for restoration through one person. Beginning with Abram, God called a people to

---

1. Gerhard Lohfink, *Does God Need the Church? Toward a Theology of the People of God*, trans. Linda M. Maloney (Collegeville, MN: Liturgical Press, 1999), 27.

live into an alternative vision for the world, to be a "unique social-project" that reflected God's reign.[2] As Lohfink notes, reflecting on Genesis 12, "God begins with very small things, not by setting the masses in motion."[3] God chose to change the world through the faith of one man.

Abraham's humble beginnings are indicated by a series of affirmations to God. He begins with yes, which reflects a trust that carries him forward until the next yes is required. Such simple affirmations constitute his step-by-step journey of faith that leads to the nation of Israel, the people of God. Through the faith of a single individual, God's plan of salvation is set in motion. While highlighting an individual's faith can sound heroic, maybe even unattainable, the narrative points not to Abraham's actions or prowess but to his trust. God chose to change the world *through* a person and a people, not *by* a person or a people. Abraham is testimony of what occurs when someone relies on God's promises.[4]

Most specifically, God redeemed the world through the person of Jesus. In biblical theology, God becoming human and dwelling among creation is referred to as *the scandal of particularity*. Universal salvation comes through a particular person in a particular place and at a particular time in history. Moreover, Jesus contradicts the messianic expectations. Even the people of Israel struggled to recognize Jesus as the Anointed One. They were looking for a universal hero, someone whose divine attributes

---

2. Lohfink, *Does God Need the Church*, 86.
3. Lohfink, *Does God Need the Church*, 28–29.
4. Lohfink, *Does God Need the Church*, 29.

would conquer their enemies and install a new political and religious order—hence the reason the temptations Jesus faced in the wilderness were so attractive. The people of God wanted a hero, and Jesus could have been it! Instead they got a Son who, like Abraham, trusted in God's promises and was faithful to God's way of small, subtle, and sometimes unassuming change in the world.[5] Only in this way could God invite creation to participate in its own redemption, to join God's household as heirs defined foremost by relationship with God.

Christians and the church today must similarly adopt a posture of responsiveness to God's call while recognizing the inherent idolatry of trying to save the world through our own perceived righteousness or power. God still calls persons and a people to be vessels, imitators, and ambassadors of God's reign, but this is only possible by relinquishing the misplaced need for power and autonomy and becoming members of God's household. Yet particularity remains scandalous to our modern desire for a universal hero. The fact that God's redemption begins with a family, a place, and an invitation to a way of life is strange, if not inconceivable. It is counter-intuitive to how we understand and expect salvation to come.

Modernity has trained us to prefer sweeping solutions and global vantage points, but something is lost when we forego handwritten directions and itineraries for global mapping and GPS instructions. Mapping is a universalizing project that invariably disregards the small things, the nuances, even the

---

5. Lohfink says, "God begins to work in the world in a small way" (*Does God Need the Church*, 40).

people and places that comprise the journey. Such a project is preoccupied with the end, or destination.[6] Responsiveness to God's call requires openness to journey while leaving the triumphal arrival to God. Only through trust in God can we disarm the hero within and replace the violent, narcissistic, and misguided epic-story arc with one of patience, peace, and ultimate assurance through God.

Obviously, before one can respond to God, God must be recognized. In God's calling of Samuel, for example, Samuel hears God but cannot recognize the voice since he does not know God (1 Sam. 3). Three times God speaks to Samuel, and three times Samuel assumes it is Eli. It takes Eli interpreting the situation and encouraging Samuel to listen more fully, with an open heart, before Samuel can recognize the voice of God. Indeed, a heart bent toward God is the starting point for knowing God. Bending one's heart toward God requires reorientation. Following the physical analogy, bending one's heart implies turning *from* and turning *toward*. Turning toward God simultaneously means turning from those competing (and ultimately fleeting) loves and desires that distract, distort, or sever our ability to find rest in God. As Lohfink states, "People are drawn and moved by that which they can desire with their whole hearts and with their whole might."[7] To know God, people must be open to "see, vividly, the beauty of God's cause, so that they experience

---

6. See Michel de Certeau, *The Practice of Everyday Life*, trans. Steven Rendall (Berkeley, CA: University of California Press, 1984). De Certeau offers an excellent analysis of modern mapping versus the nomadic encounters discovered in the pilgrimage journey. See Part III, "Spatial Practices," and chapter 9, "Spatial Stories."
7. Lohfink, *Does God Need the Church*, 47.

joy and even passionate desire for the thing that God wills to do in the world."[8]

Unlearning the heroic storyline can open us to recognize God anew. In some cases, we may come to know God as we have not known God before—more deeply, more fully. That is the gift of going home and finding true rest. The anxious, epic, universalizing narratives that are so prominent today are placed in perspective next to the people, places, and real things of this world. At home with God we rediscover that God is proprietor and savior of the world—not us. Our role, as John Wesley states, is to be stewards, or servants, of that which we are given. There is nothing heroic about stewards, yet there is "no character that more exactly agrees with the present state of [humanity] than that of steward," Wesley states.[9] Though contrary to our expectations of power and change, God has chosen to redeem the world in small, subtle, unassuming ways. God continues to call a people, just as God called Abram and his family, to steward a new way of life in the world. God's way is not characterized by dominance, coercion, or universal acts of strength. There is no point pouring new wine into old wineskins (Mark 2:22). This new way has always been and continues to be the kenotic way of Jesus: the way of self-emptying, of becoming a servant and humbling oneself to be an ambassador of God's reign.

---

8. Lohfink, *Does God Need the Church*, 47.

9. John Wesley, "Sermon 51: The Good Steward," *John Wesley's Sermons: An Anthology*, ed. Albert C. Outler and Richard P. Heitzenrater (Nashville: Abingdon Press, 1991), 419.

Cultivating the Holy Life

In Western cultures, change is often described as an act of *making*. This description is especially prevalent in recent centuries as Western societies reflected changes brought by the Industrial Revolution. There is great confidence in the human ability to *make* things and little patience for things that take time to *cultivate*. We have become accustomed to how so-called technological advancements enable immediate gratification. "Progress," we have been told and have come to believe, is marked by a type of freedom from the pains of work and the pressures of time. Apparently, humans have been liberated from toil, from waiting, and from delayed satisfaction. While Western thinking tends toward *making* change, many Native American and Eastern cultures utilize agrarian imagery to describe change. As Parker Palmer noted, "I once heard Alan Watts observe that a Chinese child will ask, 'How does a baby grow?' But an American child will ask 'How do you make a baby?'"[10]

Interestingly, agrarian imagery is also the dominant imagery of the Hebrew and Christian scriptures. The notion of *making* in Western societies derives from patterns that are ingrained deep in our reliance upon manufacturing, inevitably shaping our communal and individual identities. A detriment to this worldview is the risk of reducing the world to mere raw material that lacks value until we impose our designs and labor on it.[11] Positively speaking, this worldview suggests confidence in the

---

10. Parker J. Palmer, *Let Your Life Speak: Listening for the Voice of Vocation* (San Francisco: Jossey-Bass, 2000), 97.
11. Palmer, *Let Your Life Speak*, 97.

human ability to make change, but such confidence needs to be appropriately restrained and kept in balance so as not to lead to a misplaced sense of self-reliance and self-assurance. Dietrich Bonhoeffer worried about the idolatrous tendencies of Western modernity. Indeed, the assumption that we can know and make (or change) all, freeing ourselves from the need of God, is akin to becoming "a god against God."[12] One does not have to wait long, Palmer notes, to hear how the word "make" infiltrates everyday speech: make time, make friends, make meaning, make money, make a living, make love.[13]

The prominence of a manufacturing worldview infiltrates the religious as well as social, political, and economic realms of society. Wendell Berry points to the dark side of how manufacturing has transformed the agriculture industry, devastating rural communities and family farming. Our attempt to make work easier, increase output, and ensure participation in the global market has come at the expense of community, culture, and craft. Rural communities and farming families are of particular concern for Berry. He has witnessed their decline since the mid-twentieth century. He fears not only the plight of local communities but also the consequences of the larger loss of human connection to land and the continued deterioration of local and collective formation. Increasingly, individuals are told they must leave home to participate in the economy. To be a productive, contributing, global citizen, one must escape their parochial upbringing and the drudgery and simplicity of their daily

---

12. Dietrich Bonhoeffer, *Ethics* (New York: Simon and Schuster, 1995), 23.
13. Palmer, *Let Your Life Speak*, 97.

lives to share in the cosmopolitan advancements of the modern world. It is a type of heroic narrative, full of allure and promise for what lies beyond. Yet this narrative rests less on a compelling vision of or curiosity about what lies ahead—less on an appeal for notoriety or accomplishment—and more on discrediting and shaming the local, the small, and the commonplace. Disconnection from home is extended beyond simply leaving a place and a people to also include disregard for and derision of that place and people. Home, in this narrative, is both unsophisticated and oppressive. Persons are taught that freedom and the opportunity to *become oneself* occurs by escape and detachment from the traditions and perspectives of their communities of origin.

This is not to discount the value of exposing oneself to other places and people or exploring the world beyond home, nor to overlook the reality that home is a dangerous and dysfunctional place for some—a place that may *need* to be escaped. Yet the modern sentiment that one's true self or fullest self only exists beyond home coincides with a Western worldview that is informed by production and manufacturing. We have to *make* something of ourselves, we are told, as though who we become is entirely a product of our own doing. Such a sentiment is likely not too different from what drove the Prodigal Son in Luke 15 to request his inheritance and leave home. He believed he needed to make a life for himself. In the process he disregarded his formation, squandering his wealth and living dissolute. Only after hitting rock bottom did he rediscover his identity and the fact that he came from and belonged to a people and a place. His life could not be of his own doing or making.

While seeing and experiencing the world beyond the nuclear family can be an important rite of passage and aid a person's maturing process, God desires movement in the other direction: a return to home. Our truest and fullest selves are found at home with God. Christians do not believe that we make ourselves holy or children of God. That is God's doing. The challenge for contemporary Christians is to separate modern notions of individual autonomy, freedom, and self-making from our Christian journeys. We are not being called to leave home but to come home and find ourselves anew in the comfort and assurance that God is creator and sustainer. God is maker, and though we are called to participate in God's creative work, we are not, despite Western inclinations, called to go out and manufacture salvation or produce redemption. As with Abraham and Israel, God seeks persons and a people to come alongside the work of God's household. Fullness for both individual persons and the world is found with God, not apart from God.

The values and patterns of modern production and consumption have become so familiar that they are now uncritically assumed. As David Foster Wallace illustrated in his speech, "This Is Water," you can't ask a fish to describe water.[14] One can't recognize what they've been immersed in until they are outside of it. The modern social and economic world is the air we breathe. Twenty-first-century trends reveal the expanded influence of modernity. The factories, assembly lines, department stores, and malls that are associated with a supposedly bygone

---

14. David Foster Wallace, "This is Water," Commencement Speech at Kenyon College, 2005.

era have only morphed into new modes of manufacturing and consumerism. We remain immersed in a culture that is built on desire and gratification, on an endless cycle of detachment and attachment and detachment again, leaving each of us yearning for the next thing.

It should not surprise us that manufacturing—as a worldview and disposition—now extends beyond the production of material things and has reconstructed the way we engage and employ information, images, language, and interactions. Even relationships are increasingly manufactured, as is blatantly illustrated by the fact that we "friend" and "follow" people on social media with the click of a button. Consistent with the culture, such interactions have become another form of consumption, and consistent with consumerism, social media platforms prey on people's needs, desires, and insecurities. Books like Jean Twenge's *iGen* and Cal Newport's *Digital Minimalism*, along with documentaries like *The Social Dilemma*, are only beginning to reveal the dark side of this industry that has been built on emotional manipulation and psychological dependence. The rapid adoption and extended use of social media signals the profound restlessness in the modern era. The opportunity to create a following and receive "likes" is incredibly attractive, if not addictive. It feeds on the misguided and unfulfilled aspects of our selves. It is no different than the myth that meaning and purpose reside in what we make and accomplish.

Miroslav Volf and Matthew Croasmun further describe what is at stake in "living in modern, fast-paced, and entertainment-saturated societies."[15] They argue that it is not necessarily that people don't know what a meaningful life is but that they are unable to pause long enough to consider what makes a life worth living.[16] To focus on questions that are fundamental to our human existence—identifying and unlearning certain modern assumptions and dispositions—remains paramount. Otherwise, the life and personhood we seek and celebrate are nothing less than misguided heroism, lacking the bearings of community, home, and authentic relationship.

What is the life worth living? How is such a life discovered and nurtured? It is not without irony that following the way of Jesus increasingly pales in comparison to other things we follow today. Maybe that is because following Jesus does not offer the immediate gratification we have come to expect in consumer society. Following Jesus—to be continually transformed into his likeness—is a process of growth in grace. Patience and perseverance are among the Christian virtues, not haste and expediency. Furthermore, Christian conversion is all-encompassing, which

15. Miroslav Volf and Matthew Croasmun, *For the Life of the World: Theology That Makes a Difference* (Grand Rapids: Baker, 2021), 24.

16. They elaborate, "David Foster Wallace describes well the predicament of people living in modern, fast-paced, and entertainment-saturated societies. It's not just that we don't know how to live meaningful lives, he says. 'We don't even seem to be able to focus for very long on the question.' With neither skills nor tools to tackle the question, we report to the habits we have learned in making consumer choices: we consult our gut feelings and some 'life projects' equivalent of consumer reports, and we decide—provisionally, for the most part, always keeping our options open. Too often our hearts, which simply want what they want and are persuaded that they would wrong themselves if they didn't get it, make the decision for us. Our only master seems to be our taste, supposedly authentically ours and yet consistently mirroring what is around us" (24).

is why most Christian thinkers, including John Wesley, describe conversion as a process or a journey. Conversion entails the whole self and is reflected in the transformation of head, heart, and hands. It is both inward and outward, and those two are inextricably connected and interdependent. What is in affects what is out, and vice versa. While restlessness expresses itself in outward forms and actions, it both reflects and continues to shape (distort) identity and personhood. In following Jesus, Christians discover that worth is not measured by what one does or makes but by who they are in relation to Jesus, the one who is truly worthy. But again, discovering worth *in* Jesus entails a process of being nurtured and nourished over time through a community and people who reflect and *in*habit life worth living—the Way of Jesus.

Western society's understanding of time confronts the needed patience and perseverance to follow Jesus. Western cultures emphasize *chronos* time—measured in linear, calculable fragments. Straight timelines of history and events, like those used in school textbooks, represent this way of seeing and engaging time. Alternatively, *kairos* time is how the Scriptures record God acting in the world. *Kairos* time underscores a fullness of time that is not bound by numerical increments. One way to distinguish *chronos* from *kairos* is to say the former is quantitative while the latter is qualitative. *Kairos* is less about production and more about meaning; less about ordering, organizing, making, and achieving and more about purpose, intent, and value.

It can be difficult to measure progress in the Christian journey, which is a disheartening reality for those trained to see results. The inclination is to identify markers, rites of passage, and levels of achievement. Churches have long created language, tools, and strata to instill a little more *chronos* in the *kairotic* journey. That impulse may be natural but is not ultimately helpful. The journey of faith is not measured by how far we have progressed or advanced. The journey is about God's grace drawing us further and deeper in. Henri Nouwen calls it a current of formation that flows underneath the external view and deep within our souls.[17] Christian formation runs contrary to the threads of modern society. It has little to do with a notion of "how far I have advanced," Nouwen writes. In fact, the journey may not even be experienced as sequential or progressive—it is about movements that "continue to call us to conversion and transformation."[18]

In responding to God's call, our transformation can often be thoughtful, slow, and reflective. It even can be (or feel) circular and meandering. Growing in Christlikeness is a patient ferment, like the slow rise of yeast activating dough. The journey is lifelong. Though we may be in a hurry, God is not. God is not inclined to the mass production of followers, as evidenced in God's character and nature in the Scriptures. God didn't opt for an assembly line when calling a people. It is no surprise that dominant images of God in the Bible include God as nurturer and cultivator, God as nursing mother, father, gardener, maker, etc. As Gerhard Lohfink writes, "God takes time, but it is not empty time."[19]

---

17. Henri J. M. Nouwen, with Michael J. Christensen and Rebecca J. Laird, *Spiritual Formation: Following the Movements of the Spirit* (New York: HarperOne, 2010), 131.
18. Nouwen, *Spiritual Formation*, 131.
19. Lohfink, *Does God Need the Church*, 29.

New Birth and *Kairos*

John Wesley's sermon "New Birth" addresses the change that occurs in the conversion process when we are born again into the holy love of God. By God's grace a total change occurs in the person, reorienting and radically altering their state of being. For Wesley, new birth entails actual transformation of heart and life. He writes,

> But as soon as he is born of God there is a total change in all these. . . . The "eyes of his understanding are opened" . . . he sees "the light of the glory of God," his glorious love, "in the face of Jesus Christ." His ears being opened, he is now capable of hearing the inward voice of God, saying, "Be of good cheer, thy sins are forgiven thee: "Go and sin no more."[20]

Wesley identifies a person's total change at new birth as one that includes having eyes and ears opened to see and hear God. Opened eyes and ears and a transformed heart show up regularly in Scripture. The ability to see is a symbol in Mark's Gospel for whether the persons Jesus encounters are open to the good news he brings. Similarly, a transformed heart—a heart of flesh rather than a heart of stone—represents the people of God and their receptivity to God's ways in the book of Ezekiel. Mark 4 references Isaiah 6:9 to compare Jesus's twelve disciples to Israel: "ever seeing but never perceiving, and ever hearing but never understanding" (Mark 4:12, NIV). Jesus's steps to lead his disciples toward transformation are revealed in subsequent verses

---

20. Wesley, "Sermon 45: The New Birth," *John Wesley's Sermons*, 339.

through his parables and his ministry. The disciples are brought to see with new eyes and hear with new ears by *participating with Jesus* in his ministry. New understanding comes through following—that is to say, in action. The gift of new birth is most fully embraced as one begins to take the steps to follow Jesus, which is the rudimentary meaning of discipleship. New birth is not limited to a one-time gift of grace. Instead, new birth occurs through a continual process of God opening our eyes and ears. In a Wesleyan sense, it is appropriate to refer to Christian transformation as an act of new birth*ing*, to indicate the ongoing nature of Christian formation.

To live into the new birth is to embrace a new way of being in the world. We surrender—indeed, we submit—our lives and our plans to God's way. In doing so, we open ourselves up time and again to God's salvation and healing of our lives and world. New birth is conjoined with repentance. There is generally a point in time or event that precipitates new birth. Christians have long acknowledged the importance of an instant or moment in which a person repents, similar to the way Jesus calls his disciples in the Gospel of Matthew: "Repent, for the kingdom of heaven has come near" (Matt. 4:17). Jesus's invitation is an opportunity for the disciples to stop, turn around, and begin anew. Turning around to follow the way of Jesus is a direct refusal of and release from all the attractions of the world. It is an act of choosing peace over violence, love over hate, life over death. The disciples' first act of turning was an event, a moment in time, but their transformation entailed a continual process of re-patterning and reprogramming. The disciples were invited to relearn how to see and hear, which included *un*learning distorted ways of living in the world that were contrary to God's ways. The Gospel accounts are full of examples of the disciples repeatedly struggling with old patterns and programming, still seeing and hearing the world in wrong ways. Should we expect any different of ourselves? Of course we struggle and occasionally revert to old ways. Transformation is a lifelong process.

When a heroic lens is levied over Christian transformation, haste and expediency replace patience and perseverance. Conversion falls prey to the modern sentiments of production and immediacy, as if we are consumers purchasing our new birth in a one-time transaction. Heroic narratives *do* retain the costly and difficult nature of being transformed. What hero achieves anything without a sacrifice? Being transformed into the image and likeness of God—holiness—via the heroic lens increasingly expects sweeping, grandiose moments, yet it is ultimately the training, the constant tinkering, and the compilation of many moments that give rise to holiness.

The holy life is a process, akin to what Kay Ryan calls our "incremental resurrection."[21] Thus, the action to "repent" or "turn around" represents a constant part of Christian transformation. It is an occurrence in which *chronos* time and *kairos* time meet. Repentance is both a singular event on one's journey that marks a new beginning *and* those multiple moments and actions that continuously propel the Christian forward into God's new way of being. Hearkening back to God's selection of and covenant with Abraham, the theme of constant repentance

---

21. Kay Ryan, "Least Action," *Poetry* (November 2003), https://www.poetryfounda tion.org/poetrymagazine/browse?contentId=42012.

and renewal is obvious. Abraham and his offspring exhibit periods of success and failure, faithfulness and unfaithfulness. Yet God's promise is unwavering. God's faithfulness is constant. Salvation is not the work of human strength or abilities. As Lohfink states, the history of salvation as represented by Abraham "arises out of repentance constantly renewed, and perhaps it is precisely the opportunity to repent and begin again like a child that keeps our world in balance."[22] New birth and being born again are acts of theological identity. Christian transformation into the likeness of Christ demands that we rediscover our belonging in and with God, becoming children of God and co-heirs with Christ. We are birthed again in God's family, under God's parentage. Despite the temptation to envision birth as a singular act and moment, as though babies are only made in the moments they leave the womb, we must acknowledge and celebrate God's constant nurturing and the infinitesimal, incremental course corrections of our lives.

Turning toward Home

Mirages, parodies, and simulacrums of our true home are ever-present and ever-tempting. We are bombarded by a cacophony of voices and barraged by distractions that tend to sever our focus on returning home with God. Maintaining focus, like keeping a navigational beacon in sight, is no easy task, and modernity has exacerbated this challenge. But to assume modern Christians face an entirely new or unprecedented challenge is a stretch. Consider Homer's *The Odyssey* and Odysseus's strug-

---

22. Lohfink, *Does God Need the Church*, 21.

gle to return home. Following the Trojan War, this remaining warrior and Greek hero seeks to return home after a twenty-year absence. Before his eventual return, Odysseus reaches a point of decision. He is a castaway on the island of the goddess Kalypso and is both her prisoner and her lover. The god Zeus commands Kalypso to allow Odysseus to depart, so Kalypso tells him he is free to go but offers him a tragic choice: Odysseus can either remain with Kalypso and be immortal, or he can go home to his wife, Penelope, and eventually die like other mortals.[23] In Homer's depiction, this is Odysseus's moment of turnaround—not too different from the Prodigal Son's realization that his father's household is his ultimate place of belonging. Odysseus chooses home and fidelity to Penelope. Maybe heroes can return home after all.

The holy life is the pursuit of rest with God. That pursuit—the journey—cultivates Christian virtues and continually transforms believers into the life of Christ. But first it requires a turning, sometimes again and again, as Christians reposition their focus and reaffirm their ultimate longing and desire to reside with God. We all have a home and can return home. That home is with God. Like God's people throughout history, our challenge remains naming and resisting the false narratives, assumptions, and distorted desires that predominate our worldview. It is time to disarm the hero within us and acknowledge the destructive tendencies of modern production, utility, and expedience. It is time to embrace the deliberate, subtle, unas-

---

23. Homer, *The Odyssey*, trans. Robert Fitzgerald, (Garden City, NY: DoubleDay, 1961), 99.

suming work of transforming ourselves and the world, recognizing that we have a God who works on the margins and quietly, from within.

three

LOCATING OURSELVES BY THE THINGS WE LOVE

‿Theologian James K. A. Smith argues that we are what we love. We have been told that we are what we eat, and we have believed that we are what we think, following the modernist view of René Descartes, who taught that humans are ultimately thinking things. For Smith, though, "'You are what you think' is a motto that reduces human beings to brains-on-a-stick. . . . Such thinking-thingism assumes that the 'heart' of the person is in the mind."[1] We cannot "think our way into holiness," Smith writes. Instead, we must start with the conviction that human

---

1. Smith, James K. A. *You Are What You Love: The Spiritual Power of Habit* (Grand Rapids: Brazos Press, 2014), 3.

beings are first and foremost lovers. We are defined not by what we *know* but by what we *desire.*[2]

We also *locate* ourselves by the things we love. Like Smith's claim, this is not a new concept. In fact, throughout the history of Christianity the church has engaged, articulated, and revised its practices and theology to help orient our affections and nurture what John Wesley refers to as "tempers" (or dispositions)—that is, our holy habits. For Wesley, the formation of our dispositions entails a formation of the heart, properly directed toward love of God and love of neighbor. In this chapter, we will engage three of Wesley's sermons to better understand the meaning of love of God and love of neighbor and its relationship to ordinary practice as essential for holiness of heart and life.

Religion of the Heart

Wesley's concern for Christian faithfulness begins with his conviction of love's transformative power for both the believer and society. Love of God and love of neighbor—which Jesus names as the two greatest commandments—provide the bedrock for what Wesley calls "true religion." Grace empowers love and makes possible true belief, which consists of trust and reconciliation and not merely orthodoxy (right thinking) and orthopraxy (right practice). Wesley's evangelical spirit drives his deep concern with how Christianity in his context had become largely intellectual and ritualized. Right doctrine and right practice are insufficient to make a Christian, according to Wesley. What is needed is "religion of the heart." Wesley once stated of ortho-

---

2. Smith, *You Are What You Love,* 7.

praxy, "Two persons may do the same outward work—suppose, feeding the hungry, or clothing the naked—and in the meantime one of these may be truly religious and the other have no religion at all; for the one may act from the love of God and the other from the love of praise."[3] Similarly, regarding orthodoxy, Wesley stated,

> A [person] may be orthodox in every point; he may not only espouse right opinions, but zealously defend them against all opposers; he may think justly concerning the incarnation of our Lord, concerning the ever-blessed Trinity, and every other doctrine contained in the oracles of God. He may assent to all the three creeds. . . . He may be almost as orthodox as the devil . . . and may all the while be as great a stranger as he to the religion of the heart.[4]

Central, then, to the eighteenth-century Methodist movement was the call for trust and relationship with God that coincides with love for neighbor. Love of God and neighbor are interdependent, with each informing and encouraging the other. Furthermore, Christians are called to an ever-deepening love that continually transforms a believer's dispositions and orients our very character toward life in God.

Wesleyan scholars often use the terms *orthokardia* ("right heart") or *orthopathy* ("right feeling") to refer to Wesley's notion of religion of the heart. These illustrate Wesley's consistent emphasis on the central role desires and affections play in Christian faith. For Wesley, true religion requires that a person's affections

---

3. Wesley, "Sermon 7: The Way to the Kingdom," *John Wesley's Sermons*, 125.
4. Wesley, "The Way to the Kingdom," *John Wesley's Sermons*, 125.

be directed toward God, thereby enabling Christian thinking and practice to be properly oriented. In other words, Wesley is not simply concerned that Christians demonstrate right affection *in addition to* right thinking and practice; rather, he is convinced that right affection is the *starting point* for right thinking and practice. The Christian call is to "renew our hearts in the image of God," and any religion that stops short of this call is "no other than a poor farce and mere mockery of God."[5] It can be said that right affection provides the bearing; it is the beacon by which Christian thinking and practice find their direction.

Many Wesleyan scholars also refer to orthodoxy, orthopraxy, and orthokardia (or orthopathy) as comprising a three-part Venn diagram. The center of the diagram is where right thinking, right practice, and right affections overlap. It represents the calling of every believer and highlights where true religion is found. While such a diagram may have its shortcomings, it is a helpful way to illustrate Wesley's emphasis on the importance of a renewed heart made possible by grace. Yet love remains the overarching paradigm for Wesley. Love of God and neighbor would stand outside—or overlay—the Venn diagram. For Wesley, love of God and neighbor is both the point and the purpose of true religion. It is its end but also its foundation—its beginning—that encourages and empowers ever deeper and more faithful thinking, practice, and affection.

For Wesley, holiness entails transformation of heart *and* life. The phrase comes from Wesley's stated purpose of the Methodist societies to "pursue holiness of heart and life." In

---

5. Wesley, "Sermon 44: Original Sin," *John Wesley's Sermons*, 334.

Wesley's own time, religion of the heart was a sorely absent component of Christian faith. His emphasis on personal renewal and inner transformation was needed in the eighteenth-century context of English Christendom, where Christianity had become so culturally normative that Wesley feared it no longer reflected its scriptural roots. Today's context is different in many respects. In the West, and particularly North America, elements of Christendom remain evident in Christianity's prevalence in societal discourse and structures, but it is a different kind of Christendom than Wesley encountered in the eighteenth century. Christianity's influence today, though equally pervasive, is unofficial; church and state are officially declared to be separate. Yet Wesley's call for "religion of the heart" is as important as ever. What would be Wesley's emphases of a religion of the heart today? Knowing that heart and life are inseparable for Wesley, what corrective to an unbalanced faith would he propose? Like Smith, he might return to the ancient wisdom of the Christian tradition and warn us that we are what we love. He might also remind us that what we love is no more a matter of what we *think* or *feel* than a matter of what we *do*—the habits and practices that display our loyalties.

Recovering the Ordinary

In 1789, Wesley began a sermon to a congregation of Methodists with the question, "Why has Christianity done so little good in the world?"[6] His audience likely presumed his

---

6. Wesley, "Sermon 122: Causes of the Inefficacy of Christianity," *John Wesley's Sermons*, 550.

question to be referring to Christianity's struggle to take root in England's multiplying colonial territories, or possibly among Muslims; or, at the very least, they may have thought he was referring to other Christians—Roman Catholic and Eastern Orthodox—but not European Protestants or the people of England. With a hint of sarcasm, impatience, and a twinge of curmudgeon, Wesley's question incited the Methodists. There is an apparent sense of discouragement in the tone of Wesley's sermon. He was eighty-six years old and had been preaching, teaching, and organizing Methodists for more than fifty years. Now, in the twilight of his life, he was admonishing the Methodists for their complacency.

Throughout his ministry, Wesley fought tirelessly against spiritualized interpretations of Christianity, and he hoped the Methodists would pave the way for Christian renewal through the witness of their lives—through their actions. Had the Methodists failed him? Had his expectations been too high? Later in the same sermon, Wesley asks, "Why has Christianity done so little good, even among . . . the Methodists?"[7] He concludes that the reason is "we have forgot, or at least not duly attended" to the calling of holiness of life.[8] Wesley had long advocated that daily practices of simplicity and neighborly love would both transform individual Christians *and* bear witness to the good news of Christ for the world.

Though untitled by Wesley, this sermon was later given the title "Causes of the Inefficacy of Christianity." Its guiding ques-

---

7. Wesley, "Causes of the Inefficacy of Christianity," *John Wesley's Sermons*, 555.
8. Wesley, "Causes of the Inefficacy of Christianity," *John Wesley's Sermons*, 555.

tion, "Why has Christianity done so little good in the world?" remains an intriguing question today, more than 230 years later. Although there is certainly a hint of discouragement in the question, there is also a sense of possibility—of expectation—of how Christian faithfulness can change the world. In this regard, Wesley's question includes at least two presumptions. First, Christianity can and should do good in the world; the gospel entails the transformation of personal and social realities. Christian faithfulness, therefore, should yield discernible positive impact beyond the church and make the world a better place. Second, Christianity *has* done good in the world, even if less than we or Wesley might hope or realize. A critical review of history tells of the successes and failures of Christian witness in the world. Indeed, in its more than two thousand years of history, Christianity has had an astonishing impact in the political, social, and economic structures of our world. Its theological presumptions and worldviews have dominated the Western hemisphere, sometimes hegemonically, and positioned both the church and individual Christians in places of oppressor and oppressed, perpetrator and victim, centered and marginalized. Along the way, Christianity *has* done good—from hospitals to education to labor laws. Christianity has paved the way for much of the positive change we have seen in the world.

Wesley's expectation that Christianity should do good in the world is predicated on his assumption that the holy life has direct implications for daily practice. His central call in "Causes of the Inefficacy of Christianity" is for Methodists not to merely preach "scriptural Christianity" but to practice it through forms of self-denial. This expectation especially meant that Methodists should resist the distorted and idolatrous love of money that encourages accumulation of wealth, and practice instead the holy love that encourages giving all one can. Throughout his ministry Wesley connected holiness to the faithful use of money, which had less to do with the "thing itself" (money) and more to do with what it meant for Christians to steward God's gifts.[9] Money simply happens to be a particularly tempting and dangerous gift. God entrusts us with many gifts, and holiness entails that we faithfully respond by employing those gifts for the sake of others. An improperly used gift is one turned inward (for oneself), which is an expression of self-love rather than love of God and neighbor.

A More Excellent Way

Wesley recognized the tendency of Christians to narrowly define gifts as the extraordinary traits of those called by God for certain forms of service. The institutional church is as culpable as any party in perpetuating a shortsighted interpretation of gifts, often limiting the term to certain ecclesial offices of clerical attributes. Wesley believed all Christians were called to use the gifts—or talents—God placed in their care to do good in the world. This was an act of stewardship for Wesley, but it was also a fundamental aspect of Christian faithfulness. The call to the holy life did not belong to clergy alone, nor should it be solely identified with extraordinary acts or attributes.

Wesley's emphasis on the importance of "ordinary gifts" can especially be seen in his sermon "The More Excellent Way," published in *Arminian Magazine* in 1787. The sermon draws

9. See Wesley, "Sermon 50: The Use of Money," *John Wesley's Sermons*, 347–57.

from 1 Corinthians 12:27–31, in which Paul notes that God has appointed "first apostles, second prophets, third teachers; then deeds of power, then gifts of healing, forms of assistance, forms of leadership, various kinds of tongues" (v. 28). Wesley is most interested in verse 31: "But strive for the greater gifts. And I will show you a still more excellent way." Wesley takes Paul's words to imply that the extraordinary gifts of the Holy Ghost should not represent the principal pursuit of Christians. According to Wesley, the first task of Christians everywhere is to attend to what he calls the ordinary gifts.

The most unique attribute of this sermon is how Wesley encourages his audience to pursue the higher path that the Holy Spirit sets before all Christians: the "heights and depths of holiness" and the "entire image of God." Readers today might expect a call to deeper holiness to cite familiar Christian platitudes like trusting God more, loving others better, or praying harder. Wesley is certainly concerned with these disciplines, but platitudes tend to become spiritualized and often fail to translate into transformed action. Wesley takes a different approach in the sermon, first bypassing the extraordinary gifts in Paul's list, the ones that are so commonly associated with Christian ministry, and highlighting ordinary gifts as the often overlooked but more fundamental calling of the Christian life. In other words, Wesley argues that all Christians should pursue holiness and that the most appropriate way to do so is not to chase the miraculous or seek the remarkable but to "covet earnestly" the transformative power of ordinary holiness.[10]

---

10. Wesley, "Sermon 89: The More Excellent Way," *John Wesley's Sermons*, 512.

And what are the ordinary gifts? In "The More Excellent Way," Wesley includes seven mundane and commonplace activities: sleep, prayer, work, food (eating and drinking), conversation, diversions, and money. Interestingly, except for prayer, which was certainly a daily practice for Wesley, the list is entirely composed of what could be called basic human activities; the concrete realities of any person's daily life. It is evident, then, that what Wesley regards as the "more excellent way" referenced in 1 Corinthians 12 has something to do with living *Christianly* in the ordinary stuff of our lives.

Yet this is not quite what Paul wrote in his first letter to the Corinthians. Paul didn't offer a list of ordinary gifts juxtaposing the extraordinary gifts he mentions. So what did Paul mean when he said, "But strive for the greater gifts, and I will show you a still more excellent way?" The answer to that question lies in the subsequent verses comprising what we know today as 1 Corinthians 13—or, "the love chapter." One of the most quoted passages of the entire Bible, 1 Corinthians 13 is known inside and outside the church; it offers an almost poetic definition of love that fits neatly into weddings and other ceremonies. Of course, Paul did not write this first letter to the Corinthians imagining *anyone*, much less twenty-first-century Christians, reading chapter 13 separately from chapter 12. The chapter-and-verse breakdowns were added hundreds of years after Paul's writing. For Paul, the end of 1 Corinthians 12 flowed directly into the beginning of 1 Corinthians 13. It would have read like this:

Now you are the body of Christ and individually members of it. And God has appointed in the church first apostles, second prophets, third teachers; then deeds of power, then

gifts of healing, forms of assistance, forms of leadership,
various kinds of tongues. Are all apostles? Are all prophets? Are all teachers? Do all work miracles? Do all possess
gifts of healing? Do all speak in tongues? Do all interpret?
But strive for the greater gifts. And I will show you a still
more excellent way. If I speak in the tongues of mortals
and of angels, but do not have love, I am a noisy gong or
a clanging cymbal. And if I have prophetic powers, and
understand all mysteries and all knowledge, and if I have
all faith, so as to remove mountains, but do not have love, I
am nothing. If I give away all my possessions, and if I hand
over my body so that I may boast, but do not have love, I
gain nothing.
(1 Cor. 12:27–13:3)

It is clear that, by "a more excellent way," Paul meant
love—but not love in a merely romantic, emotional, or abstract
way. In 1 Corinthians 13, Paul describes love as patient, kind,
not envious, boastful, arrogant, or rude; not self-seeking, irrita-
ble or resentful; not rejoicing in wrongdoing but in the truth (vv.
4–6). What Wesley does, by highlighting ordinary gifts in his
sermon, is provide for his audience a bridge between 1 Corinthians 12:31 and 1 Corinthians 13: love is embodied in concrete
and tangible ways, even mundane ways. The love Paul describes
is a daily love that is bound to basic human interactions and
activities. Simply put, love is performed daily—which is not to
say it is easy, but it doesn't require grand gestures or heroic acts.
Love does not demand extraordinary gifts. It is fundamental
for all Christians. It is the foundation of the life of holiness and
central to Christianity's witness in the world.

Though anachronistic, placing Wesley's sermons "Causes of the Inefficacy of Christianity" and "The More Excellent Way" next to each other exposes a common thread. Wesley was concerned that early Methodists were falling into the trappings of the broader societal and ecclesial contexts. Methodists were increasingly enamored of the extraordinary and were beginning to interpret holiness and the Christian life through something akin to a heroic lens. But they were supposed to be the church's renewal movement, a people who exhibited an alternative vision of Christian faithfulness driven by love of God and neighbor. Why had Christianity done so little good in the world? And even the Methodists? They had forgotten their first love.

(Ordinary) Holiness: Rooted in Love of God and Neighbor

In some ways, it is ironic to identify Wesley as a promoter of the ordinary among Christians. Wesley himself was extraordinary, and is lauded today as everything from scholar to saint to organizational genius. As is often the case with such persons, their lore and legend grow in the generations that follow. We can't help but make them into heroes. Nevertheless, in his own life Wesley promoted a vision of holiness that was grounded in everyday Christian life. There was nothing particularly novel about it. John Wesley was shaped by a long history of Christian thinkers and innovators who challenged the prevailing constructs of Christianity in their time. In the fourth century, John Chrysostom confronted Christianity's acquiescence to power, naming the elitism of his day and raising the significance of everyday faithfulness among ordinary Christians, especially the poor. In a broad sense, monasticism did the same thing—particularly Benedictine monasticism, which undercut the pursuit of wealth and political power by giving priority to the communal over the individual and celebrating holiness in everyday activities like labor. Thomas à Kempis provided a similar challenge to the status quo at the height of Western Christendom in the late medieval period. Notably, his book *The Imitation of Christ* helped Christians rediscover the task of holiness and emphasized the virtues of simplicity and humility. Wesley was deeply impacted by Chrysostom, Benedict of Nursa, and à Kempis.

In this sense, Wesley's concern for ordinary holiness is both a reiteration and repackaging of those who preceded him. In fact, he is unabashed in drawing from the wisdom of previous thinkers and parallel circumstances in Christian history. In a different sense, Wesley is unique. His eighteenth-century context—marked by both a culturally comfortable Church of England and involuntary Christianity (*i.e.*, birthright Christianity), and the expanding colonialism and industrialism of England—required an unparalleled degree of leadership, innovation, and critical evaluation for a renewal movement to gain a foothold. Wesley possessed the traits and qualities needed to challenge the ideals of power, wealth, and privilege that were inherent in his context. He also had the theological depth and creativity to counter misassumptions and propose alternative constructs of Christian faithfulness.

Contemporary elevation of the extraordinary in Christianity is nothing new. Nor are we without a long history and deep tradition of alternative visions of Christian faithfulness. Drawing from our Wesleyan roots, we can affirm that what should define any Christian seeking transformation of heart and life is neither pursuit nor obtainment of extraordinary gifts but instead pursuit of a right heart and faithful practice of ordinary gifts for the sake of others. In this regard, attending to the ordinary is a necessary and practical part of discipleship. A right heart and ordinary practices are intertwined and interdependent. Most of us know that what we do (and how) is shaped by what we love or desire. Our many choices and activities each day reflect what we love and value. Yet, as noted at the beginning of this chapter, what we love is also largely shaped by what we do. There is a symbiotic relationship between what we love and what we do; each informs the other. Wesley knew that the shaping of a right heart—true love of God and neighbor—depended on Christians engaging in practices that would ultimately form holy tempers and affections. Wesley referred to such practices as the "means of grace."

Wesley describes the means of grace as "ordinary channels" through which God conveys prevenient, justifying, or sanctifying grace.[11] Such ordinary channels are potentially limitless because God's grace can be discovered and encountered through various avenues and interactions, many of which are commonplace. Wesley does, however, qualify the means of grace as "outward signs, words, or actions ordained of God."[12] This definition certainly includes the sacraments but also entails practices like visiting the sick or almsgiving—acts of neighborly love. In fact, Wesley distinguished between *instituted* means, *prudential* means, and *general* means of grace. Andrew Thomp-

---

11. Wesley, "Sermon 16: The Means of Grace," *John Wesley's Sermons*, 160.
12. Wesley, "The Means of Grace," *John Wesley's Sermons*, 160.

son explains these categories as follows: *Instituted* means of grace refer to those means established by Jesus in the Gospels. Wesley highlighted five instituted means of grace as prayer, Scripture, the Lord's Supper, fasting, and Christian conferencing (or fellowship). *Prudential* means of grace entail practices or patterns that are reflective of Christian wisdom and context. The organization of Methodist classes and bands and practicing the works of mercy are fitting examples. *General* means of grace are the habits and attitudes that draw us into God's presence. Denying ourselves (fasting), keeping the commandments, or "taking up our cross" (Matt. 10:38; 16:24; Mark 8:34; Luke 9:23) are ways that Wesley understood we could be drawn closer to God.[13]

When Wesley published his sermon "The Means of Grace" in 1746, he was concerned about the hesitation many Methodists exhibited toward established Christian rituals and practices, seeing them as unnecessary or potentially detrimental to their faith. Wesley could identify and even sympathize with concerns of rote ritualism, having engaged similar sentiments among the Moravians and other quietists.[14] Nevertheless, he maintained that the means, when used "as ordained [and] not for their own sake," were purposeful for "the renewal of [the] soul in righteousness and true holiness."[15] In the sermon, Wesley outlined three primary means of grace: prayer, Scripture, and the Lord's Supper. We have already noted that

---

13. Andrew C. Thompson, *The Means of Grace: Traditioned Practice in Today's World* (Franklin, TN: Seedbed Publishing, 2015).

14. Outler and Heitzenrater, "An Introductory Comment," *John Wesley's Sermons*, 157.

15. Wesley, "The Means of Grace," *John Wesley's Sermons*, 170.

Wesley included prayer in his list of ordinary gifts, alongside food (eating and drinking), sleep, work, conversation, diversions, and money. Wesley understood prayer as a common element of the Christian life. Similarly, he believed that reading and reflection on Scripture and partaking of the Lord's Supper should be commonplace activities in the Christian life. Regarding the latter, Wesley even devoted an entire sermon to his claim that "it is the duty of every Christian to receive the Lord's Supper as often as [they] can."[16]

So, although Wesley categorized the means of grace and even found himself consistently defending the ordinances established and administered by the Church of England, he was steadfast in his conviction that the means of grace are "ordinary channels." They are ordinary as in, plain and readily available, but also in the expectation that Christians engage them on a regular—even daily—basis. In this regard, Wesleyan-Holiness and Methodist churches have long emphasized works of piety (e.g., prayer, Communion) and works of mercy (e.g., feeding the hungry, visiting the sick) as common practices of the Christian life. The works of piety and works of mercy convey God's grace, deepening both personal and social holiness. In this regard, the means of grace shape whom and how we love. Wesley understood these ordinary channels to have the power to foster our love and understanding of God—which, of course, overflowed into love of neighbor and care for the poor.

---

16. Wesley, "Sermon 101: The Duty of Constant Communion," *John Wesley's Sermons*, 502.

The Small Things

In attending to the ordinary, we attend to what we love. Emphasizing ordinary holiness is a way of recognizing the needed reorientation of our loves because what we love and what we do are inextricably connected. But a right heart takes time and practice, and holy living takes a right heart. Wesley knew this. The lure of the extraordinary is often the lure of the shortcut, the temptation to jump ahead, to gratify, to solve, and to save by foregoing the painstaking work of getting there. The lure of the shortcut was partly Jesus's temptation in the wilderness, and it's the opposite of the work of patient ferment. Interestingly, superheroes never seem to have to practice much. They reflect our great yearning to jump ahead to success and triumph. But we "common ones" must exercise the power of habit, which is ultimately a gift because lasting differences are made in the little things.

Many are familiar with the oft-cited ten-thousand-hour rule: that mastery of a skill requires ten thousand hours of practice. Malcolm Gladwell popularized this standard in his *New York Times* bestseller *Outliers*. He identifies ten thousand hours as the "magic number of greatness," a common "tipping-point" when a person achieves high proficiency or expertise in a subject or skill.[17] The specifics remain a topic of debate, but the general concept that practice makes perfect remains widely accepted. Should we expect it to be different for the transformation of heart and life? Do not sanctification and growth in grace re-

---

17. Malcolm Gladwell, *Outliers: The Story of Success* (New York: Back Bay Books, 2013).

quire, as Wesley put it, the "working out our own salvation" in response to the work of God?[18]

Gladwell's *Outliers* tells stories of success and how achievement is made possible through hard work and practice. Holiness should not be equated with *achievement*, as though our human capacities alone enable us to realize some terminus of perfection. Holiness is about God's work in and through us but also with us. As Wesley says, "First, God works; therefore you can work. Secondly, God works, therefore you must work."[19] While we should not equate holiness with achievement, we could say that holiness includes *acquisition* in the sense that we acquire virtues through practice. Much like Paul notes of love in 1 Corinthians 13, the expertise of love—or, the acquisition of that virtue—comes only through the daily practice of the attributes of love, over time, for a lifetime.

Most of us do not think about *how* we learn. We may recognize that we have learned something, and we are generally able to recall key moments or practices in the learning process. We might note "aha" moments, when we came to a realization or the practice we put into learning a skill or subject. We know learning takes time. Learning to see the world through the eyes of Christ—discipleship—takes time too. The temptation to expedite undermines the learning process, and despite knowing that learning takes time, we still struggle to be patient.

---

18. See Wesley, "Sermon 85, On Working Out Our Own Salvation," *John Wesley's Sermons*, 485–92.

19. Wesley, "On Working Out Our Own Salvation," *John Wesley's Sermons*, 490.

When we were helping our first son learn to read, we discovered the power of habit—the daily exercise of him reading with us and then to us. At first, we were concerned about him understanding the rules of language, how to sound out words and recognize punctuation and sentence structure. We were eager to teach him *how* to read, as though in a moment it would all just click, as though he would jump from level-one reading to chapter books overnight. Attempting to teach these things to our son was both overwhelming and unsustainable. Then we realized what mattered, what actually made a difference: consistent practice. In the end, it was our nightly ritual of reading, every day, no matter the circumstance, no matter how tired. The ritual instilled understanding in ways our teaching could not. Learning is always a process. Geniuses and prodigies may demonstrate advanced natural or intellectual abilities, but mastery itself has no shortcuts.

In a similar way, I can attest from both personal experience and from working with hundreds of students that, despite the occasional or momentary success one may achieve in cramming for a test, cramming information is not a sustainable or effective way to learn. Deep understanding of a subject and the practical wisdom that follows takes time. It demands not only head knowledge but also ownership and understanding in the heart and hands. A good learner is not defined by their GPA but by their *sapiential* knowledge—knowledge that is characterized by wisdom. "Teaching to the test" is a common approach under the pressures of standardized testing. Tests like the SAT, LSAT, and GRE measure, as much as anything, one's ability to prepare for and master a test. If only *love* could be consolidated to a test. If only the complexities and nuances of life and relationship could be boiled down to a set of testable maxims. Let us thank God that this is not the case, however messy that means love must be. Learning to love, especially to love well, takes time. It is a virtue, like wisdom that is acquired through practice. We cannot *cram* our love of God and neighbor.

Just as Wesley recognized the temptation among early Methodists to fast-track love of God and neighbor, he also saw the danger of what we would today call *moral licensing*. Moral licensing acknowledges that individuals may grant themselves permission to act less ethically or responsibly following a good deed or significant ethical act. Moral psychologists have shown this behavioral tendency to be quite common, for example, with individuals' eating, exercise, and consumer habits. But it can go beyond simply allowing myself to have ice cream as a reward for exercising. Moral licensing has much more to do with allowances than rewards, which is how it can foster immoral or irresponsible action when it comes to a person's or institution's responsibility to care for the poor or marginalized. In these cases, one good deed becomes the justification for a series of misdeeds. A classic example, from Wesley's sermon "On Visiting the Sick," is when a wealthy person sends a medical doctor to someone who is ill, in lieu of visiting the sick themselves. While one could justify the effort as more immediately necessary, it also undermines the means of grace that could have possibly been shared between the sick person and the potential visitor.[20]

---

20. Wesley, "Sermon 98: On Visiting the Sick," *The Works of John Wesley, Volume 3: Sermons III (71–114)*, ed. Albert C. Outler (Nashville: Abingdon Press, 1986), 387.

What makes moral licensing especially challenging to address is that individuals are generally not cognizant of their licensing. In this same vein, John Wesley was disturbed by the early Methodists' apparent lack of concern for ordinary holiness. When enamored of grand gestures and extraordinary acts, it's easy to forego Christian responsibility in the small and consistently difficult work of neighborly love. Wesley advocated for the continual practice of the works of piety and mercy, partly to counter the human tendency to regress in our growth of holiness. Interestingly, Wesley doesn't give near the same attention or advocacy toward extraordinary acts or experiences in his ministry. Even his revivalist spirit is tempered by his method. For Wesley, holiness never came in one fell swoop. Nor does changing the world come through our grand gestures and extraordinary acts. Christianity can do a lot more good in the world if, as Wesley suggests, we recover ordinary holiness. It is not heroic; in fact, it is mundane. But in the small things we nurture our love of God and neighbor and create a sustainable foundation for lifelong transformation. The effect is cumulative and born from consistency and perseverance.

Consider the analogy of brushing teeth. For most of us, brushing our teeth is habitual. We were taught to care for our teeth at a young age and were instilled with the daily practices of flossing, brushing, mouth-washing, gargling, and perhaps other acts of oral hygiene. From a historical perspective, widespread daily tooth-brushing was not prevalent until the mid-twentieth century. It took advocacy and popularization of the practice for it to be established. Young children remind us of how peculiar tooth-brushing can seem until the habit is established. Our youngest son, at four years old, said he didn't need to brush his teeth one day because he had brushed extra-long the day before. The logic is understandable. Why brush your teeth twice a day for one minute when you could brush once a month for sixty minutes? The former is mundane, but the latter would feel sensational, if not heroic. We'd pat ourselves on the back, post pictures of our teeth to Instagram, and tell others about our amazingly fresh breath. Once that gratification wore off, we'd probably give ourselves license to have a few teeth-rotting candies. Gross, right? Gross because we know that wouldn't do much good. A sixty-minute tooth-brushing marathon (and go ahead and throw in flossing and mouthwash) would grant only a momentary high and offer little discernible impact toward long-term wellness. Tooth-brushing must be habituated. There is nothing heroic about it, but its cumulative value is undeniable.

Wesley wanted a Christianity whose impact in the world was undeniable. He also wanted a holiness that was ever-deepening and growing in maturity. While the pursuit of holiness may be marked by moments—the holy surprises and experiences that shape a journey—transformation comes through the accumulation of the little things. In the little things, the ordinary stuff that comprises our lives, we develop our character and offer our allegiances. In the little things, we solidify our affections and establish our dispositions. In the little things, we have the opportunity to right our heart, and in so doing, right our thinking and doing in ways that extend beyond ourselves for the flourishing of the world. No wonder Wesley, before all works of piety, said to visit the sick and offer charity.[21] Through such works of mercy our loves, and thus our lives, become properly ordered.

---

21. See Wesley, "Sermon 92: On Zeal," *John Wesley's Sermons*, 465–73. Wesley states, "Thus should he show his zeal for works of piety; but much more for works of mercy. . . . Whenever, therefore, one interferes with the other, works of mercy are to be preferred. Even reading, hearing, prayer, are to be omitted, to be postponed, 'at charity's almighty call'—when we are called to relieve the distress of our neighbour, whether in body or soul" (469).

PART II

Postures of the Holy Life

It is time for all the heroes to go home
if they have any, time for all of us common ones
to locate ourselves by the real things
we live by.[1]

---

1. Stafford, "Allegiances."

We all, unavoidably, live by real things. The simple and seemingly mundane rhythms of day-to-day life are essential to human thriving and the created order. Yet the modern inclination is to deny the power of the daily, and to escape. So we define the world and its interactions by the extraordinary rather than the ordinary, the exceptional rather than the commonplace. In doing so we forget that who we are is ultimately shaped by our regular practices and performances—the stuff we live by. In the commonplace, lives are shaped and changed. That is not to say that holiness, embodied and experienced, is simply a set of mastered practices, codes, or rules. Holiness is a way of life. It shapes practice and is shaped by practice. Ultimately, holiness remains instantiated in affections and dispositions, as one's way of being is transformed into Christlikeness.

Chapter 3 identified how what we do shapes what we love. The Christian journey is located, in large part, by habituated affections and dispositions; by that which we seek and desire and work toward. Practices nurture and nourish our affections and dispositions—which is why Wesley believed it was important that the people called Methodists engage in specifically Christian practices in order to cultivate Christian virtue. Works of mercy and works of piety are prime examples of practices that bolster the Christian journey, promote holiness, and reorder the narratives through which we read the world.[2] It takes time for practices to do their work. Mastery is not acquired overnight. Muscle memory, intuition, and tacit knowledge become eventu-

---

2. For more on how narratives inform our interpretation of the world, see James K. A. Smith, "Nothing outside the Text? Derrida, Deconstruction, and Scripture," *Who's Afraid of Postmodernism? Taking Derrida, Lyotard, and Foucault to Church* (Grand Rapids: Baker Academic, 2006), 31–58.

al trademarks of every master. Aristotle acknowledges this when he writes that "moral virtue comes about as a result of habit."[3] Wesley went so far as to note that even the ordinary, mundane practices of everyday life (such as eating, sleeping, and more) shape believers in the way of holiness when they are engaged as participation in God's redemption.

There are, of course, numerous practices that shape Christian virtue and holy living. Rather than point to or explicate a specific set of practices, which is undoubtedly an important task, this section proposes three *postures* that are essential for recognizing and responding to the ordinary gifts encountered on the Christian journey. A posture—a stance, position, or attitude—highlights the ways Christians might face, encounter, and interact with the world. The postures proposed are not exhaustive, but they counterbalance the challenges of modern, and particularly Western, Christianity. Rediscovering these postures is essential, given the frequently misguided state of contemporary Christian journeys.

Practices themselves are adaptive and fluid. When faithful to a tradition and an overarching narrative, practices reflect and embody their past while attending to and responding to new contextual realities. Postures can inform practice. Rote, ill-informed, or ill-intended practices are ineffective, if not detrimental to, the holy life. A proper posture that is grounded in the assurance of God's sustaining and redeeming power and in our kinship in God's household is the bedrock and starting point for faithful practice.

---

3. Aristotle, *Nicomachean Ethics*, trans. W. D. Ross (350 BCE), Book II:1, http://classics.mit.edu/Aristotle/nicomachaen.2.ii.html.

The postures of voluntary displacement, wonder, and walking humbly offer guidance and stability for the wayward and restless. They can help Christians regain their bearings, more easily decipher distorted images of holiness, and recover an authentic Christian presence in the world that witnesses to God's reconciliation of all things. These are not heroic postures and should never be embodied as acts of glory or self-aggrandizement. Preferably they are ordinary: subtle, small, unassuming. Modern heroes frequently miss precisely what is needed to discover peace in their own lives and in the world they seek to change. Stafford's concluding stanza illuminates the answer: we each must "locate ourselves by the real things we live by." We must not fear—in fact, we should embrace—being common: with places, people, and a home in God. In doing so we are defined not by what we think or what we say but by how we live. As Thomas à Kempis once said, "The kingdom of heaven does not stand in words [and, we may add, ideologies], but in good, virtuous works."[4]

---

4. Thomas à Kempis, *The Imitation of Christ* (Garden City, NY: Image Books, 1955), 165.

four

VOLUNTARY
DISPLACEMENT

A posture of being displaced, voluntarily, should sound odd given this book's emphasis on seeking home and locating oneself spiritually and even physically in a place and with a people. Yet there is value in choosing to reside outside the comforts, securities, and privileges afforded by home. Displacement reorients the way we see the world and even our presumed homes. For Christians, voluntary displacement remains an essential part of our pursuit of home with God. It helps dispel false notions of home that may be more cultural or consumerist than theological and enables discovery of unique and diverse expressions of rest with God. Displacement helps Christians relinquish presumptions and engender new imagination for what it means to belong to the household of God.

Home is a complex concept in the twenty-first century. Human experiences and expectations of home are exceedingly diverse. One may associate home with kinship or bloodline or perhaps extend it to an immediate, blended, or intergenerational family. Home, therefore, becomes much more than a physical space. For others, home may be no more than an illusion, abstract but never experienced, or simply a construct of the human species like a pack, herd, or group of animals that provides order and ensures safety and survival. For all, home—or its absence—is marked by culture and is undeniably part of who we are and how we see the world. In this regard, even the Old Order Amish—who are known for their tight-knit communities and clear emphases on place and family—have long understood the significance of leaving home. Amish communities are known in popular culture for maintaining the tradition of *Rumspringa*. Although this term originated merely as a way to reference the period of adolescence, it has taken on a larger meaning in American society, fueled by media attention, and has come to symbolize parents allowing their children, usually around the age of sixteen, to consider leaving the community. After the *Rumspringa* period, the teenager or young adult can decide whether they want to be baptized in the Amish church and commit themselves to the Amish life.[1] In this case, voluntary (and temporary) *dis*placement lends to voluntary (and permanent) placement; the Amish community is composed of those who choose to be part of that people, place, and tradition.

Voluntary displacement should also sound strange when we consider our increased awareness of global migration. Refugees,

---

1. For more, see Richard T. Schaefer and William W. Zellner, *Extraordinary Groups: An Examination of Unconventional Lifestyles*, 9th ed. (Long Grove, IL: Waveland Press, 2015), 39–80.

asylum seekers, immigrants, and internally displaced persons may not have homes to return to, or their lives may be marked by the necessity of displacement for survival. Globalization has given rise to peoples on the move and the reality, for some, of lifelong displacement. On average, a refugee will spend fifteen years in a temporary camp. Many displaced children have known no other home than the refugee camp. Clearly the harsh realities of forced displacement stand in direct contrast to the freedoms others are afforded due to wealth, privilege, or social location. It is important to acknowledge that home, place, and belonging are more than walls of brick and mortar and more than family origin or history, which for many can carry its own mix of disappointment and misunderstanding. Home, theologically understood, is our center and hub. It grounds us in God and God's desired intentions for the world. Only this home can enable us to be who God has created us to be.

Voluntary: Openness to Something New

Alongside the inhuman realities of forced migration and displacement, globalization has also given rise to the explosion of geographical and cultural tourism. The motivations and experiences of the tourist stand in contrast with those of the pilgrim. The tourist cannot shed the cosmopolitan gaze. They remain a consumer of experiences and cultures that are deemed "other" because the tourist "goes in search of the exotic."[2] Even borders and boundaries retain importance to the tourist because they

---

2. William T. Cavanaugh, *Migrations of the Holy: God, State, and the Political Meaning of the Church* (Grand Rapids: Eerdmans, 2011), 78.

reaffirm the tourist's own distinctiveness and difference. They offer distinction between the modern and the pre-modern, the developed and the underdeveloped. As William Cavanaugh aptly notes, "The tourist gaze depends on borders to maintain the kind of difference that it craves."[3] In contrast, pilgrimage is an ancient model of mobility that "is not dependent on the imperial gaze," nor does it draw its motivation from the self.[4]

The motivation for the pilgrim is neither consumeristic nor self-serving. Pilgrimage, properly understood, is an act of discipline, meaning an act of surrender or openness to God's instruction. Pilgrims also travel for penance, seeking the forgiveness of sin, and occasionally not out of their own volition but at the demand of the religious community. The difference between tourists and pilgrims for encountering the world reflects distinct postures toward self and others. While the tourist desires escape from one place and people in order to experience, albeit momentarily, another place and people, they never fully shed their securities or relinquish their comfort. The tourist's worldview is inevitably expanded through new encounters but is also, ironically, truncated then reified by the shortsighted and frequently privileged position of their viewpoint. In essence, tourists never get outside themselves. They are never displaced to the point of having to see the world in a new way. A pilgrim's journey, on the other hand, is not self-serving. The pilgrim seeks self-transformation and to broaden their perspective and better attune their life with God's, but the ultimate purpose of pilgrimage is trans-

---

3. Cavanaugh, *Migrations of the Holy*, 77.
4. Cavanaugh, *Migrations of the Holy*, 79.

formation *for the sake of the world.* As such, the pilgrim's displacement is an act of self-emptying and surrender to God—an openness for God to do something new. Accordingly, pilgrimages are intentionally open-ended journeys that remain attentive to unexpected, holy encounters that enlighten the pilgrim and even redirect the journey. While tourists consume the journey by controlling itineraries and collecting novelties, pilgrims surrender themselves to the journey and thus are consumed by it.

The distinction between tourist and pilgrim is important because both typically engage their journeys voluntarily. "Voluntary" implies agency and freedom. It can also reflect modern notions of individuality and autonomy and suggest a degree of wealth or power by which one is afforded the privilege to choose. Indeed, voluntary denotes the possibility of some self-determination and actualization. Tourism does not entail displacement in the same way pilgrimage does, and for a posture of voluntary displacement, *voluntary* signifies an intentional or purposeful conviction to encounter new vantage points and embark on a journey of transformation for the sake of the world.

*In*voluntary displacement would, of course, include forced migration and persons seeking asylum, refuge, or economic stability, but it can also include displacement that is driven by rote obligation or the generic social pressures that are the consequence of modern heroism. With the latter, a person can be displaced for the wrong reasons—often from a compulsion for social advancement, or vainglory. Such displacement is ultimately destructive for the self and for others since it precludes the desire to be wholly formed into God's reign.

At this juncture in Christian history, it is paramount that voluntary displacement be enacted by those who have long been afforded a seat at the table through their implied power and privilege while others have been overlooked, or "othered," because of gender, class, race, or ethnicity. Power and privilege must be named and surrendered so that those who have become accustomed to their presumed superiority can truly see and honor the lives of others. Voluntary displacement promotes transformation into a child of God. It spurs awareness of dependence on God and others in a life that is not defined by power but by following the way of Jesus that is so radically different than the world yet is known to be our salvation.

God still often works in and through involuntary pilgrims. Jonah is a quintessential example. His reluctance and self-centeredness interfere with his calling, almost costing the lives of his shipmates and the people of Nineveh. But God intervenes, and God's purposes are fulfilled. Jonah struggles to shed his smugness. Even as Nineveh repents, Jonah wallows in sanctimonious self-pity. While Scripture testifies that God will see God's purposes fulfilled, the involuntary pilgrim foregoes the opportunity for self-transformation. Throughout the Bible, kings, prophets, and disciples who are unwilling or unable to set aside their egos, control, or preset expectations frequently fail to attain or experience God's ultimate aims. In fact, many whose displacement was initially voluntary later struggle as they grow weary or lose sight of God's purposes. Moses, Saul, David, Judas, and Peter are all but a few obvious examples. Yet each is also a reminder that God can work through us and despite us even when we become complacent in our comforts and lose our way on the journey. Similarly, when a disciple or prophet voluntarily yields to God's direction in the Bible—though never without God's urging—incredible things happen. Persons like Ruth, Jeremiah, John the Baptist, and Paul reflect a unique willingness to travel open-ended paths and be used in unforeseen and unexpected ways. They are reminiscent of the faith of Abraham who "set out, not knowing where he was going" (Heb. 11:8b).

Reorientation: Seeing Others

The term *narcissism* derives from Narcissus in Greek mythology. Narcissus was a hunter known for his beauty whose self-obsession became his downfall. In the story, Narcissus falls in love with his own reflection in a pool of water. He spends his days unable to stop staring at himself and dies frustrated that he could not materialize his self-created image. As a personality disorder, medical diagnoses of narcissism (NPD) are relatively rare, but the more general struggle of self-absorption is all too common. Humans are prone to narcissistic tendencies, which are often driven by personal insecurities and the need for self-adulation to compensate. The story of Narcissus is a simple but compelling portrait of human propensity. Even organizations and communities can become self-absorbed with maintaining their image or materializing an unobtainable ideal.

The story of Narcissus functions as a fitting juxtaposition to a posture of voluntary displacement. Bent over, tunnel-visioned, and finding false security in one's own reflection inhibits persons from seeing and receiving the world around them. One can imagine Narcissus, so comfortable in his gaze that he becomes complacent, neglecting his changing environment and his bodily need for food and water. Displacement, on the other hand, forces a new perspective. Even the slightest change of position would have adjusted what Narcissus saw in the pool. A few degrees in angle may have been enough to help Narcissus notice the beauty around him: the trees on the side of the pond, the sun setting, a fish just under the glare of the water, or Echo, the talkative nymph who loves Narcissus and mourns as he wastes away in self-infatuation.

Windowpanes provide a similar illustration and have been employed in literature and art to address the complexity and significance of changing vantage points. Depending on the lighting, angle, and type of glass, windows offer either a mirror effect or a lens to see the world on the other side of the pane, and sometimes a little of both. Even as a window enables one to see through to the outside, it often simultaneously produces some reflection back to the viewer. In this regard, a window can be clouded and prevent full sight. In fact, a person looking through a window may not initially see the persons or objects on the other side but only his or her own reflection, which raises questions about clarity: What do people truly see? Do they see through the window to others and the world? Or is the window opaque and clouded by the image of oneself?

Voluntary displacement entails creating new vantage points to ensure we see ourselves and the world around us in new ways. Although narcissists may be self-absorbed to the point of neglecting everything beyond their own image, we can all grow overly content when we gaze at anything from a fixed position. Displacement changes the angle, casts light differently, and adjusts the field of vision, offering new information to the brain about what is seen and experienced. Without changes in perspective, Christians can easily become complacent, hearing but not understanding, seeing but not perceiving (Matt. 13:14). As Frederick Buechner writes, "When Jesus comes along saying that the greatest command of all is to love God and to love our neighbor, he too is asking us to pay attention. If we are to love God, we must first stop, look, and listen for him in what is happening around us and inside us. If we are to love our neighbors, before doing anything else we must see our neighbors."[5]

We are accustomed to placing ourselves at the center. Our inclination is to see and interpret the world around us as though the axis on which the earth spins is wherever *we* are and whatever *we* experience—hence, the significance of the common phrase "this isn't about you." It is natural to internalize the challenges or pain of those around us, and it is certainly important to be in solidarity with those who suffer. But intervening out of our own needs—not the *actual* needs or best interests of others—is a prototypical heroic temptation. The savior complex drives people to see themselves at the center of everything. Inevitably, they turn the stories of others into their own stories. They appropriate others' experiences and, in so doing, deny others' personhood and uniqueness. Like children, we could all occasionally use the familiar parental reminder, "The world doesn't revolve around you." Taking a step back, or to the side, is vital to rediscovering God and the Spirit's movement at the center of all things. The Christian task is to get on board with what God is up to in the

---

5. Frederick Buechner, *Whistling in the Dark: An ABC Theologized* (New York: Harper and Row, 1988), 16.

world, which requires overcoming the temptation of thinking that the primary thing God is up to, or the primary agent in what God is up to, is *me*.

In this regard, recovering the practice of hospitality is especially important for twenty-first-century Christians. The practice of hospitality has a rich history in the Christian tradition. When it is not practiced thoughtfully or faithfully, however, it can support tendencies to not fully see another and to approach the other with a sense of privilege, dominance, or superiority. But when it is practiced faithfully, hospitality opens Christians to the hard work of empathy, placing ourselves in another's situation. Hospitality includes removing ourselves—our desires and presumptions—from the center in order to make space for the perspectives, experiences, and hopes of others. In its fullness, Christian hospitality welcomes the guest to the point of no longer being other or outsider. In fact, a great reversal happens, an inversion of relationship, where the guest becomes the host. The divisions between insider and outsider, haves and have-nots, center and margin, become dismantled.

The notion that hospitality is simply the act of sharing from one's abundance and making *a little* space for the other is insufficient. That truncated version of hospitality fails to engender transformation since the host never has to relinquish power or control. Following the window analogy, it is as though the host never has to shift from the center and therefore never gains new perspective. Christian hospitality is the act of those at the center availing themselves to become guests in God's dynamic world. Others—often seen as outsiders in need of our gifts—are invited to share *their* gifts. The former host is now the recipient, discovering and embracing new gifts from the world beyond their previously narrow vantage point.

Hospitality that opens itself to host displacement and the gifts and vantage points of others is decidedly Christian because it represents a living testimony of trust in the fullness of God. To surrender one's securities and control and open oneself to alternate vantage points is an act of Christian confidence in God's redemption and salvation of the world. The alternative to a posture of displacement is a posture of fear, as personified by hosts who are unable to receive gifts from others. Intended or not, fear becomes a statement about God that reveals one's ultimate hope and trust not in God but in oneself. Fear declares that God is not in control. Fear drives the narcissist deeper into their gaze as they live with increasing certainty that the salvation of the world requires (or revolves around) them.

Displaced Locally

In a world where we are trained to find comfort and solace in consumption—of experiences, people, places, and things—and in having the freedom to discard those very things when they lose their novelty, being *placed* is a type of displacement. Placing oneself—that is, committing to a community, environment, and its people and rhythms—runs counter to the modern preoccupation with individual autonomy and solitary heroes. To connect to a people and a place and to seek to be a compassionate and contributing member of a community confronts the comfort and security we have been taught to find through escape and impermanence. Choosing to stay—or at least living like you are not leaving—is hard work.

A friend and former professor Doug Harrison once shared advice he received from his superior at a L'Arche community.[6] As Doug's time as a volunteer came to an end, he began, inevitably, to disconnect from community members. This tension is a common challenge for any who serve and get assigned or called elsewhere. The human instinct to avoid pain is strong. Yet, as Doug pulled away, his superior confronted him and encouraged him to embrace his current place and time and not to distance himself by jumping mentally and emotionally into the future but instead to "work toward your hardest goodbye." Doug chose to remain *placed*, despite his pending departure. His decision contradicted the narratives and inclinations of the modern self. It was surely uncomfortable. Detachment would have been easier; he could have shifted into visitor mode. But that would have disabled him from continuing to truly see, experience, and be transformed by others in the L'Arche community.

Indeed, the modern proclivity for detachment turns the gifts of a place and people into commodities. As Walter Brueggemann stated of modern placelessness: "That promise concerned human persons who could lead detached, unrooted lives of endless choice and no commitment. It was glamorized around the virtues of mobility and anonymity that seemed so full of promise for freedom and self-actualization. But it has failed. . . . It is *rootlessness* and not *meaninglessness* that characterizes the current crisis. There are no meanings apart from roots."[7] Volun-

---

6. L'Arche communities are intentional communities that are devoted to ensuring care and belonging for persons with intellectual or developmental disabilities.
7. Walter Brueggemann, *The Land: Place as Gift, Promise, and Challenge in Biblical Faith* (Philadelphia: Fortress Press, 1977), 3–4.

tary displacement engenders a host of robust yet commonplace Christian practices. Practices that help fulfill the command to love one's neighbor are a prime example. Persons who embody a posture of voluntary displacement are more likely to engage others in simple yet meaningful and consistent ways.

Traditional forms of neighbor dependence and support have diminished in modern societies. With ease of access to information and home goods, we rely less on our neighbors for news, that extra sack of flour, or their tools and expertise in mending fences or fixing roofs. Neighborhoods are rarely communities anymore, but rather geographically situated social contracts. Neighbors in the typical North American context generally respect each other's rights and privacy, and band together to define and uphold a shared sense of living standard. In this regard, relationship with neighbors is functional, like a transaction. But a Christian sense of neighborliness goes beyond the status quo and opens new possibilities. Small acts of sharing meals, borrowing tools, and even requesting a neighbor's help (imagine that!) have the profound capacity to promote friendship and neighborly bonds. Engaging in those acts—not just with neighbors who think and look like you—further represents a posture of voluntary displacement.

Rest assured that, in developing bonds with neighbors, you will find people you do not agree with, maybe even do not approve of. You will learn their stories, how their experiences have shaped them, and maybe even how you play a role, whether directly or indirectly, in their flourishing or hardships. Ultimately you will discover that they need you, and you them—first to water plants, then to watch pets while out of town; eventually for an emergency, and then in recognition that our fullest selves are realized in shared life with others. Such neighborliness requires true openness to God working in and through other persons. It demands not only an obvious relinquishing of self-centeredness but also a willingness to set aside heroic tendencies of grand gestures and universal impact to give our attention, instead, to the common, lived realities of the persons God has placed on our journey. Admittedly, modern Christians have not always made the best neighbors. For many clergy, when the average tenure at an assignment is three to five years, it remains difficult to embrace place. And for all Christians captivated by heroic narratives, it seems there are always bigger and more important things to do than attend to the real things people live by. It is easy to become so fixated on saving the world that we neglect the persons God has placed directly in front of us.

Slowing down and serving one's neighbor, like the Good Samaritan, is an act of voluntary displacement. The Good Samaritan had to surrender his own plans and timeline for his day. He had to set aside his own agenda and, in aiding the beaten man on the side of the road, open himself to an unknown future. Will the man require medical attention? Will he have a family who needs to be notified or may need support? Will he be violent? Did he *deserve* to be beaten and robbed? It is never hard to rationalize avoiding the risk of insecurity and discomfort, as illustrated by the priest and the Levite in the Parable of the Good Samaritan (Luke 10:25–37). But as the Christ hymn reminds us, being transformed into the likeness of Christ entails looking not to one's own interests but to the interests of others; to emptying oneself for the sake of others (Phil. 2:4–8).

five

WONDER

℘"Let the little children come to me, and do not stop them; for it is to such as these that the kingdom of heaven belongs" (Matt. 19:14; Mark 10:14; Luke 18:16). These words of Jesus that are found in each of the Synoptic Gospels parallel similar statements of his that emphasize the upside-down nature of God's kingdom and the uplifting of the overlooked or marginalized in human society. Jesus's statement about children is frequently interpreted to underscore the value of simple faith. This interpretation is fitting so long as *simple* is not equated with *naïve* or *ignorant*, as if faith does not entail seeking understanding or as if simplicity is a state of perpetual bliss.

God delights in our curiosity and desires our inquiry and interest. It is an act of worship to stand in awe of God. Wonder is a recognition of our own createdness and God's omnipotence, omniscience, and omnipresence. Wonder demonstrates awareness that we are participants in God's story, yet we are active participants who seek to uncover our role, place, and function in the storyline. In Greek, the words "household" (*oikos*), "economy" (*oikonomia*), and "world" (*oikoumene*) share the same root, reflecting the Greek understanding of social structure. For Christians, God's household, God's commonwealth, and God's reign (kingdom) are similarly related. Children naturally seek their role, place, and function in a household. A healthy household provides a safe, affirming place for a child, but it also offers identity, purpose, and belonging. Like children, God invites us to discover not only who we are but also how to fully participate in God's redemptive purposes for the world. Discovery begins with questions. Like children, we must not be afraid to ask why, and we should watch intently—as children often do with their parents or guardians—for clues of what a reconciled and redeemed creation looks like. As the apostle Paul writes, "all who are led by the Spirit of God are children of God" (Rom. 8:14). We have "received a spirit of adoption" (v. 15) and are "heirs of God and joint heirs with Christ" (v. 17).

Juxtaposed with the child are the scribes and Pharisees. "Woe to you," Jesus says several times in Matthew 23, classifying them as hypocrites and blind guides. Their religious fervor is not in question—only their certainty, their self-righteous piety, and their obliviousness to the movement of God's Spirit in the world. They are the embodiment of those who know and trust only the law as written on stone and cannot comprehend the intended *meaning* of Jesus's teachings in the Sermon on the Mount. There is an apparent distinction between a follower of Jesus and a Pharisee, between a curious child and a self-assured adult who has settled into a version of truth or perspective that prevents them from seeing God in new and unexpected ways. Often the desire for certainty and security can too quickly override curiosity. The curious remain open—not naïve, ignorant, or blown willy-nilly by the latest "-ism"—but open to the fresh, unfolding work of God in the world.

Play

The nineteenth and twentieth centuries saw a resurgence of post- and premillennialist teachings in Christianity. These teachings fixate on the thousand-year reign of Christ that is referenced in Revelation 20. Premillennialism grew in popularity following the American Civil War, and it differed from postmillennialism in that it did not seek to usher in Christ's thousand-year reign but instead waited for Christ's return as the inauguration of his thousand-year reign. Both types of millennialist teaching emphasize the heroic narrative that salvation can be brought about for humanity *by* humanity. This misdirected focus deadens the church's capacity to see Christ himself breaking into history anew. Millennialist teachings make the mistake of assuming we are the center of the world and that we have or can discover the key to the world's future. In a strange reversal, it becomes Christians—not God through Christ—who save, or who at least precipitate salvation.

The pre- and postmillennialist battles of the last two hundred years are indicative, again, of the long-standing infatuation with the heroic myth and the temptation within humanity to assume that both creation and its restoration are dependent on us. Christians must pave the way for Christ's return (postmillennialism), or we must save sinners in preparation for Christ's return (premillennialism). Both make God's salvific work contingent on human action. Both move Christ to the periphery, making him largely an agent of some future redemptive work instead of an active agent of God's salvific grace in the world already. In many ways, modern Christianity is plagued with over-seriousness. Culture wars, ideological battles, and even violence have been employed to advance one version or another of truth. In such instances, the world looks on in dismay while Christian witness loses its potency.

It is not difficult to see divine commands in the Bible to battle cosmic forces and establish God's reign. Similarly, God clearly desires a people who take with utmost seriousness love of God and neighbor, pursuit of holiness, and work toward a social order characterized by Christ's lordship. It is also abundantly obvious in Scripture that God's people are called foremost to worship God. Worship entails practice—the active embodiment of God's reign—but it first demands awe and reverence. Worship rests on the awareness of God's sovereignty and greatness; the recognition that God is Creator and we are creation. Twentieth-century theologian Karl Barth challenged the temptation in his own time to overemphasize humanity's role in the redemption of the world. Such overemphasis not only displaced the central function of Christ as testified in Scripture but also reified a false pretense of human correlation with God. For Barth, humans are called to participate with God in the salvation of the world, but "this does not mean that [the human] becomes a co-creator, co-saviour, or co-regent in God's activity. It does not mean that [the human] becomes a kind of co-God."[1]

---

1. Karl Barth, *Church Dogmatics III.4: The Doctrine of Creation*, trans. A. T. Mackay, T. H. L. Parker, H. Knight, H. A. Kennedy, and J. Marks, ed. G. W. Bromiley and

Human work can be "active participation [to] the service of the kingdom" but remains limited as "creaturely activity."[2] The Wesleyan perspective offers a bit more optimism than Barth's for the human capacity to live into God's redemptive purposes, but it too stands squarely on a distinction between God and creation, between Savior and saved.

Barth posits that Christians should embody playfulness like that of children. Human work—not mere employment, but all the stuff that comprises "the active affirmation of human existence"—can become idolatrous when not seen in proper relation to God's work.[3] In fact, human work measured alongside the work of God "cannot be anything but play . . . a childlike imitation and reflection of the fatherly action of God which as such is true and proper action."[4] This reality does not make human work meaningless. On the contrary, placing human work in relation to God's work increases its seriousness, just as when "children play properly . . . they do so with supreme seriousness and devotion."[5] Therefore, Barth contends, "we are summoned to play properly."[6] We must avoid the temptation of taking ourselves too "terribly seriously" and recognize that, "even at best, we cannot be more than children engaged in serious and true play."[7]

T. F. Torrance (London: T&T Clark International), 482.

2. Barth, *Doctrine of Creation*, 482.

3. Barth, *Doctrine of Creation*, 527.

4. Barth, *Doctrine of Creation*, 527.

5. Barth, *Doctrine of Creation*, 527.

6. Barth, *Doctrine of Creation*, 527.

7. Barth, *Doctrine of Creation*, 527.

The Gospel account of Jesus visiting Mary and Martha illustrates Barth's point. After Martha welcomes Jesus into her home, she gets engaged in "her many tasks" (Luke 10:40), presumably those of hosting. Meanwhile her sister, Mary, "sat at the Lord's feet and listened to what he was saying" (v. 39). Martha is bothered by Mary's apparent indifference and says to Jesus, "Lord, do you not care that my sister has left me to do all the work by myself? Tell her then to help me" (v. 40). Jesus responds, "Martha, you are worried and distracted by many things; there is need of only one thing. Mary has chosen the better part" (vv. 41b–42a). Much has been made of this passage throughout Christian history, including justification of a longstanding sentiment to see labor, particularly manual labor, as inferior to the contemplative life.[8] Alternatively, this passage neither addresses labor nor denounces the importance of Martha's work but acknowledges the common snare of missing the point. It is not, as Martha contends, Mary who is sidetracked by Jesus; instead, Martha is preoccupied by her own sense of haste and busyness. She is taking herself and whatever goals or outcomes she has for the visit too seriously. Mary, on the other hand, exemplifies a disciple who is open to Jesus's presence. She sits as Jesus's feet in awe and curiosity; she measures her purpose in relation to his.

As individual Christians, we have Martha and Mary moments scattered along our journeys. Often, we are fixated on what we presume to be the most essential, important, or expect-

---

8. Early monastics and, later, Thomas Aquinas are especially illustrative of the long-held Christian emphasis on the superiority of contemplative life over the active life.

ed. Our perspective gets truncated by the tasks at hand: solving a crisis, building a program, sustaining an institution. Other times we encounter Jesus in new ways. The circumstances or our posture and God's constant seeking enable us to sense the movement of the Spirit. In those moments, we are most truly who God has called us to be: children at play, summoned to play properly, imitating—that is, intently listening/watching—and reflecting God's work in the world.

Holy Wrestling

In 1986, Daniel Taylor wrote the influential book *The Myth of Certainty*. His thesis—which was desperately needed in its time and is still crucial today—challenged the general close-mindedness and disdain toward doubt that has been characteristic of modern Christianity. For many Christians, questioning one's faith or belief is tantamount to sin. Having a faith that can move mountains (an image we get from the Gospels—see Matt. 17:20; 21:21) became virtually synonymous with having an unshakable faith (which has no biblical precedent). Subsequently, to question, doubt, or wrestle with faith was shameful. I know no mature Christian who has never doubted or questioned God, but few feel the freedom to voice those questions; few are comfortable being open about their doubts. Taylor's work spurred greater acknowledgment of and appreciation for the place of questioning in faith.[9] God, who desires

---

9. A more recent text that can be especially beneficial for young adults is Jeffrey F. Keuss, *Live the Questions: How Searching Shapes our Convictions and Commitments* (Downers Grove, IL: IVP Books, 2019).

our worship, seeks our free, full, authentic love. Worship that is blind, coerced, or ignorant is not worship. It is at best a rote performance and at worst a dishonest offense to the God who created us with the capacity to reason and feel.

Christian discipleship often focuses on the unwavering faith of biblical heroes. There is indeed value in highlighting the awe-inspiring certainty and perseverance of a servant of God. But how many young Christians *only* know of Moses, Elijah, or David in their best moments, by their grand acts of confronting Pharaoh, calling down fire, or slaying a giant? The other side of those heroes' journeys is less frequently discussed and tends to be reserved for mature Christians and the quiet corners of Christian teaching. There is wisdom to not beginning with the heavy stuff, but maybe the reluctance to name the doubt, the wandering, and the occasional unfaithfulness of biblical predecessors has something to do with how their struggles are all too real. We have much to learn from a Paul who grows weary, a Thomas who doubts, a Peter who succumbs to self-preservation, a Job who is angry, a Jacob who wrestles, and various prophets who question and lament.

Wrestling especially needs to be recovered as an expression of Christian faith and worship. Jacob's wrestling at the place he later names Peniel represents a turning point in Jacob's journey and has profound allegorical significance for the people of God (Gen. 32:22–30). Because Jacob persevered, he is blessed and given the name Israel, which means "you have striven with God and with humans, and have prevailed" (v. 28). The people of Israel, as well as the Christian church that shares in the same promise and calling (Rom. 11), can also be referred to as those who engage in holy wrestling. God desires a people who follow not out of fear or ignorance but as an act of worship. To question, explore, and even doubt are expressions of reverence and awe toward God. Might God celebrate the curious atheist over the uncritical conformist? To worship, love, and be in covenant with a God on the move—a missional God—entails a readiness *to be moved*. To wrestle with God is to engage God. God is not threatened by our wrestling. In fact, in Jacob's story, the mysterious person approaches and provokes Jacob. Scripture remains a testimony of the paradox that the God who is Wholly Other seems uninterested in being a divine autocrat and instead welcomes creation into partnership.

Frederick Buechner calls the story of Jacob's wrestling the "magnificent defeat" in his book by that title. Reflecting on Buechner, Ronald Rolheiser states that to wrestle God and come out unharmed, one would perceive to have won the blessing. The point of the story, however, is that Jacob comes out with a permanent limp. To live with a limp is a sign that one's own strength has been defeated—yet the blessing is still given. Thus, Rolheiser explains, "The blessing for which we are forever wrestling can only come to us as gift, not as something we can snatch through our own talent, cunning, and strength."[10] The 'permanent limp' is that sign and signal that our seeking depends not on ourselves, but in relinquishing ourselves to God.

---

10. Ronald Rolheiser, "A Magnificent Defeat," June 8, 2020, https://ronrolheiser .com/a-magnificent-defeat/#.YUoEY7hKgzx.

Daily Wonder

A posture of wonder is expressed in various tangible ways. Fundamentally, wonder influences daily interactions, not only with others but also with oneself and the world. Like ripples on a pond when a stone is thrown in the water, embracing wonder at the core of our being has levels of exponential effect. While the rippled-pond analogy suggests one-directional impact (moving outward), the ripples are ultimately interconnected, playing off one another even if our naked eye only catches the ever-expanding rings. Similarly, wonder is not siloed. Like an inclination or disposition, it reflects one's way of being, and what wonder opens and exposes is never isolated to specific places, moments, or people. Wonder infiltrates. Like an immune system that is boosted by antibodies, wonder helps fend off the fear of change and lack of confidence in God's sovereignty that can easily mutate into the diseases of self-righteousness and egotism.

The modern world has attempted to free itself from nature by dominating it in order to ensure that our comforts, securities, and agendas would not be affected by changing seasons, weather patterns, or other natural barriers. Consider our twenty-first-century dependence on climate-controlled environments, uninterrupted and increasingly speedy travel, and engineered microclimates like many green agricultural zones in the southwest United States. Modernity has been more about control than wonder, more about ruling the environment than being subject to it. But in freeing ourselves from nature, we have become sheltered from it and have forgotten that we are dependent upon and intertwined with its very rhythms. For maybe the first time in human history, persons who are so busy with the bustle of life can fail to notice the changing of a season, can miss the oddity of eating a strawberry or a banana in the dead of winter, and can ignore the fact that their water and power supplies come from the mass harnessing of natural forces. Such things are not necessarily bad, but they are illustrative of the particularly modern predicament that our desire for sovereignty over nature dispossesses us of the *gifts* of nature. In our attempt to rule creation, we can miss the beauty of being *part* of creation.

Celebration of the change of seasons entails the transformation of more than simply our exterior or physical environments. For example, after a long winter of cold temperatures, bare trees, and brown grass, spring offers new vantage points and marvels of life. Seasons mark life-cycle changes, each one birthed by infinitesimal shifts. The numerous and miniscule changes can easily go unnoticed, especially when our lives are less connected to and dependent on the land. Yet increasing our awareness of the little things can profoundly impact our relationship with God and others. God placed humans within the ordering of creation, and we are our fullest selves when we live within its rhythms. As Parker Palmer writes, "Spring teaches me to look at life carefully for the green stems of possibility."[11] What emerges may be no more than a whisper, yet it is a precious gift that only watching eyes and listening ears will capture. Palmer notes that the possibilities found in the smallest movements of human life can create large change—maybe a glance or a touch that

---

11. Palmer, *Let Your Life Speak*, 104.

thaws a frozen relationship.[12] In awakening our senses, we also cultivate the patience to be fully present.[13] Engaging our physical bodies in the world around us opens us to new imagination and possibility. In so doing, we reject the dualistic mindset that tempts us to believe spirituality can somehow be separate from the physical world we inhabit—as if the act of thinking itself is not something we do *in our bodies*. Those who have nurtured the art of increased awareness and presence with God's creation benefit from a greater spectrum of experience of God. Expanded recognition of the gifts of God supports greater receipt of and response to those gifts. Through wonder the still, small voice of God can ring loud: maybe in the quiet of a field, the glow of the moon, or the dancing of birds through the trees. Such awareness, Palmer suggests, counteracts the noise and busyness of our lives and opens us, over and over, to "the stranger's act of kindness that makes the world seem hospitable again."[14]

Wonder changes the way we see and interact with others. Recognition of the dynamic nature of God's creation supports awareness of the beautiful complexity of human community and the symphonic nature of truth. One does not have to be musically inclined to be fascinated by what happens through the collective craft of a symphony orchestra. Even an untrained ear can recognize and appreciate the varied functions and sounds of different instruments. Seeing them at a live event certainly helps. To the untrained, many musicians and instruments can go

---

12. Palmer, *Let Your Life Speak*, 104.
13. Palmer, *Let Your Life Speak*, 104.
14. Palmer, *Let Your Life Speak*, 104.

unnoticed and unappreciated when listening only. *Seeing* them evoke curiosity. What does that instrument do? What sound or role does it play in the whole? Similarly, attuning our ears to the contributions of others requires constantly seeking to *see* the other—their experiences, their perspective, their unique though maybe subtle gifts.

Twentieth-century theologian Hans Urs von Balthasar's love of the symphony prompted his book *Truth Is Symphonic*. In it, he describes the collective work of truth through the beautiful interweaving of sound that takes place in the symphony:

> Symphony means "sounding together." First there is sound, then different sounds and then we hear the different sounds singing together in a dance of sound. A bass trumpet is not the same as a piccolo; a cello is not a bassoon. Each one keeps its utterly distinctive timbre, and the composer must write for each part in such a way that this timbre achieves its fullest effect. . . . In the symphony . . . *all* the instruments are integrated in a whole sound. . . . The orchestra must be pluralist in order to unfold the wealth of the totality that resounds in the composer's mind.[15]

Symphony is a re-creation of sounds timed in unison. Not only are these different sounds "sounding together," but there are also juxtaposed, contradicting, and conflicting sounds woven to create the tonal storyline of the music. Composers know well that harmony requires dissonance as well as consonance. There must be sounds of tension and clash to establish the interweaving

---

15. Hans Urs von Balthasar, *Truth Is Symphonic: Aspects of Christian Pluralism*, trans. Graham Harrison (San Francisco: Ignatius Press, 1987), 7–8.

themes of a harmonious drama. Wonderers avail themselves to hear and appreciate these symphonic subtleties. They learn to see past the occlusion of uniformity and find richness in the pluriform and pluriphonic. Even in a cacophony of sounds, a melodic line can present itself, and sometimes it takes discordance to uncover new harmony.

Although a trained musician is better equipped than the average person to recognize and orchestrate symphonic sound, Balthasar's analogy includes everyone. If truth is symphonic, then God intends us to discover the polyphonic potential within our communities and all of creation. Most of us can begin by truly *seeing* the other and learning to recognize their contributions. Only then do we begin to *hear* differently, appreciating the subtleties of difference and even discord. The temptation is to ignore, deny, or silence different sounds for the sake of coherence and cohesion. This pragmatic compulsion flows from a realism that tells us that strength depends on clear order and lack of deviation. For human communities, though, denying difference disregards the work of God in and through the other. It is also indicative of hidden idolatry—the presumption that we already possess the truth, which is a type of rejection of God and a fraudulent misrepresentation of our own role as God's children, God's people, and God's creation. The conductor and instrumentalists in an orchestra know they are not the composer. Their purpose is to bring forth the wealth of the composer's work through the integration of all the instruments.

On a personal level, wonderers exhibit a profound capacity to embody what the Peace Prayer commonly associated with St. Francis of Assisi requests: "to not so much seek to be consoled as to console, to be understood as to understand, to be loved as to love." Wonder helps counter self-focus. The needs to be recognized, to be respected, to be right, to give advice, to defend, and to justify become increasingly irrelevant as attention is turned toward God and others. Awe and curiosity press persons to see past themselves, to ask how or why, to empathize rather than criticize.

Contemporary Christians ought to reflect on the admonishments of the peace prayer. It is not easy to give preference to the other or to truly seek another's welfare over one's own. Embodying this prayer is especially hard in a world where ample avenues have been created to circumvent the virtues of patience, charity, and temperance. Social media, for example, rarely engenders wonder and, worse, tends to intensify personal perceptions. Despite social media's occasional value of increasing awareness, platforms are largely echo chambers used to further solidify the perspective of a person and their collective interest group. Local congregations and even denominations can suffer from similar misdirection, becoming places to contend for certain cultural and political identities—social interest groups rather than faithful expressions of the gospel of Christ.

When holiness is foremost defined as management and control of sin, we miss God's invitation to participate in the goodness of creation. Holiness entails distinction. To be sanctified is to be separated and consecrated for God's purposes. However, it does not mean—as the church mistook at times in its history—that Christians condemn, avoid, or escape the world or that our call is to establish an enclave. Instead, God calls a people to be a new paradigm *in* the world and witnesses to God's reconciliation and redemption. Sadly, Christianity is popularly viewed as a faith tradition that is bent more toward control than openness, that is more interested in its own enclave than it is in engagement with the needs of the world. Recovering wonder can counteract this misinterpretation of personal and corporate holiness. Wonder is about explaining less and pondering more. Propositions must give way to confessions. *I confess*, meaning, *I don't fully understand, but I believe; I trust.* To live with an openness and expectation of ever-abounding newness is unmistakably Christlike. Jesus sat with sinners, emptied himself for the sake of others, and submitted himself to God's will. Not surprisingly, Jesus would have preferred an alternative route: "Father, if you are willing, remove this cup from me; yet, not my will but yours be done" (Luke 22:42). Even Jesus wonders—curious and possibly puzzled by his pending crucifixion as the salvific act and archetype of a reconciled world. Indeed, wonder is built into the very framework of God's created order.

six

WALKING HUMBLY

"He has told you, O mortal, what is good;
and what does the Lord *require of you*
but to do justice, and to love kindness,
and to walk humbly with your God?"
—Mic. 6:8

The evangelical tradition, emerging in early Pietist and Puritan movements in Britain, gave heightened attention to personal faith and Christian action. John Wesley's threefold emphasis on orthodoxy, orthopraxy, and orthokardia (right thinking, right practice, right loving) as constitutive of Christian faith resembles commitments of the broader early evangelical movement.[1] Early evangelicals helped recover within Christianity the indelible connection between head, heart, and hands.[2] Following the scholastic period and the doctrinal developments of the Prot-

1. Wesley, "The Way to the Kingdom," *John Wesley's Sermons*, 123–31.
2. Consider David William Bebbington's "evangelical quadrilateral," first proposed in *Evangelicalism in Modern Britain: A History from the 1730s* (London: Routledge, 1989). Bebbington's list includes biblicism, crucicentrism, conversionism, and activism.

estant Reformation, renewed attention on religion of the heart and religion of the hands was sorely needed. Modern inheritors of evangelicalism further advanced these commitments, at times even over-stressing heart and hands to the detriment of head. Os Guinness's famous treatise *Fit Bodies, Fat Minds* highlights the consequence of latent anti-intellectualism in Pietism and related fundamentalist movements of the twentieth century.[3] Leave it to American evangelicals to treat their bodies as temples but their minds as compounds, walled off from external influences and critical engagement.[4]

An overemphasis on heart and hands, however, can extend beyond a suppression of the role of the mind in Christian faith and undermine Christian virtue and character. Disregarding the mind stunts our moral formation by detaching thought from action, context from belief, and community from confession. Christian thought has a vital function in practical moral reasoning. Holiness Movement emphases on sanctification as personal and instantaneous, for example, can inadvertently relegate the practice of seeking and discerning God's will, which hinders the work of consistently articulating, then acquiring, the Christian virtues. In such cases it is helpful to be reminded of Paul's words that with the new covenant in Christ a veil does not lie over our minds. The veil, like that which covered Moses's face, has been removed. There is now freedom to see (or "contemplate," in some translations) the glory of the Lord and be "transformed into the

---

3. Os Guinness, *Fit Bodies Fat Minds: Why Evangelicals Don't Think and What to Do about It* (Grand Rapids: Baker, 1994).
4. See also on this subject Mark A. Noll, *The Scandal of the Evangelical Mind* (Grand Rapids: Eerdmans, 1995).

same image" (2 Cor. 3:18; see vv. 15–18). Paul does not see the mind as an obstruction but as a facilitator of Christian transformation. The removed veil enables us to contemplate God and discern the character of holiness.

The evangelical recovery of the importance of heart and hands and heightened fervor to live out kingdom ethics in the world is to be commended. Renewed emphasis on the holistic nature of the Christian faith and personal and social transformation remains vital today. One challenge is for modern evangelicals to avoid the theocratic temptations of early Puritans who frequently attempted to make the entire social order "Christian," sometimes by coercion. Sadly, throughout history Christians have frequently behaved badly when they've had too much political or social power. Even so, Micah 6:8 corresponds with the modern evangelical spirit. Do justice, love kindness (or mercy), and walk humbly. For half a millennium, evangelicals have nurtured a profound awareness and conviction to *act* and *do* in the world, sometimes even hastily in attempts to instill the world with justice and mercy. Less recognized is the call to walk humbly—not as a personal pietistic challenge but as a posture or disposition in the world. Walking entails acting and doing, of course, but frequently overlooked is how walking humbly with God is more about *being* than *doing*, more about finding rest than running a race.

Indeed, Micah 6:8 provides a succinct reference to what God expects of God's people. It is quotable, challenging, and in many ways reflective of the tenor of the whole of Scripture. To walk humbly with God is a primary virtue of God's people. The proud and lofty will be made low and humble (Isa. 2:12), and

Jesus even parallels humility with faithfulness when referencing the "weightier matters of the law: justice and mercy and faith[fulness]" (Matt. 23:23). Of course, in the context of Micah 6:8, the meaning of the Hebrew word *leket*, "to walk," suggests *living* humbly. Humility can be characterized as the embodied practice of God's people, a habituated posture that is formed through obedience to and admiration of God. It is more than an outward expression, worn like a piece of clothing; it is the result of complete transformation, permeating the very way we carry ourselves in the world.

The Virtue of Humility

What might it mean to *be* humble as opposed to simply *act* humble? What if humility is not just a performance to accomplish something else—a means to an end—but the end itself, the very purpose of God's people? In this regard, God is less interested in a people who can don a cloak of virtue and more interested in a virtuous people. The difference becomes apparent because only the latter fully submit to and place trust in God's redemptive work. Only the latter exhibit ultimate confidence in God's authority over the powers and principalities of the world, as exemplified in Christ. The truly humble relinquish the need to control and know their place in God's story.

Among the classic atonement theories is a version of the ransom theory championed by Gregory of Nyssa, sometimes referred to as the fishhook. In his analogy, Satan is tricked by accepting the humanity of Christ (the bait) as a ransom for sin. Satan assumes he is victorious in Christ's death, but really he has only swallowed the hook (Christ's divinity). Satan is then defeated. The analogy has multiple flaws, including a heretical differentiation between Christ's human and divine nature and the unsettling assumption that Satan has some dominion or authority over humanity that God can only resolve through trickery. To the current point, though, the fishhook analogy also contradicts Jesus's embodiment of humility that is attested to in the Christ hymn. It turns humility into a tool or an instrument whose sole purpose is to trick the devil. Jesus was never *actually* meek, nor was he required to empty himself, as Philippians 2 testifies. He was never truly the Lamb that was slain—he was just a wolf in sheep's clothing.

It is easy to identify and criticize the theological contradictions that emerge from Gregory of Nyssa's fishhook atonement theory. It is much harder to recognize the ways that contemporary Christians practice and propagate similar contradictions. Humility (or meekness), along with the other Beatitudes (Matt, 5:1–12) is fundamentally a disposition—a way of being in the world. Embodying these dispositions is the primary calling of God's people. Our pragmatism and impatience tempt us to shortcut God's timing and work. We wonder how the Beatitudes can be *useful*, either as a way of earning or establishing the kingdom of heaven or heaping burning coals on others' heads (Rom. 12:20). Yet Jesus does not simply offer the Beatitudes as a way *to* the kingdom but as the way *of* the kingdom. Those who are poor in spirit, who mourn, who are meek, who hunger and thirst for righteousness, who are merciful, who are pure in heart, who are peacemakers, and who are persecuted are the blessed ones who, like Jesus, incarnate and embody the kingdom of God on earth.

But, like for Gregory of Nyssa, meekness makes more sense to us as an instrument or a ploy. We prefer power and yearn for an epic battle or heroic climax. We prefer Jesus's triumph over death be announced with blasting trumpets, toppling kingdoms, and repenting sinners. But what we get in the Gospel accounts of Easter Sunday is mistaken identity, marginalized women, and fearful disciples. Even in this moment of Jesus's resurrection—the fulcrum of history—God continues to move in small, subtle, unassuming ways. The humility that defines Jesus's nature and led him to the cross is not discarded following his emergence from the tomb and triumph over death because humility was never a means to an end for Jesus. It was never a tool or an instrument. It was certainly not a trick. Instead, humility is a core attribute of the image of God, and it is an attribute Christians must increasingly embody if they are being transformed into God's image.

The Christ Hymn is commonly cited beginning with Philippians 2:5, "Let the same mind be in you that was in Christ Jesus." The two preceding sentences, verses 3 and 4, establish humility as the hymn's guiding virtue, so it is appropriate to cite the entirety of the hymn along with verses 3 and 4:

> Do nothing from selfish ambition or conceit, but in humility regard others as better than yourselves. Let each of you look not to your own interests, but to the interests of others. Let the same mind be in you that was in Christ Jesus,
>
> who, though he was in the form of God,
> did not regard equality with God
> as something to be exploited,

but emptied himself,
taking the form of a slave,
being born in human likeness.
And being found in human form,
he humbled himself
and became obedient to the point of death—
even death on a cross.

Therefore God also highly exalted him
and gave him the name
that is above every name,
so that at the name of Jesus
every knee should bend,
in heaven and on earth and under the earth,
and every tongue should confess
that Jesus Christ is Lord,
to the glory of God the Father.
(Phil. 2:3–11)

For Western Christians emerging from the ashes of Christendom
arrangements where Christians and the church have exercised
significant power over social, economic, and political spheres,
verses 3 and 4 are a clarion call. Humility—more than purity or
duty or power—needs to be recovered as the essence of Christian holiness and the guiding image of the transformed life. Of
course, it will do no good for Christians to underscore or claim
humility pretentiously. In this case, humility requires confession,
which should be less an act of verbal profession and more a form
of service and repentance. In any context where Christians have

abused their privileged position, humility necessarily entails self-emptying.

Understanding humility as an embodied and primary virtue of the people of God corresponds to the word's etymology. Humility is related to the Latin *humilitas,* associated with being from the ground or earth. In English it is related to *humus,* referring to the soil. Associated words like earth, ground, and soil clearly identify humility as an expression of being lowly and basic—the ordinary stuff of creation. The Christian practice of imposing ashes on foreheads on Ash Wednesday—generally accompanied by some variation of the words, "Remember that you were formed from dust, and to dust you shall return"—is a tangible rehearsal of humility. In this practice, Christians remember our place as God's creation, our lowly status, and our need for God's salvation. While death is undone on Easter—a seeming reversal of our pending status as ashes—our place in the commonwealth of creation is not. Ash Wednesday remains an appropriate reminder that we belong to God and that, much to our anthropocentric dismay, God's restoration of all things does not ultimately depend on us. In this sense, the calling of God's people to be humble entails a recognition of our own lowliness—our creatureliness—and our fundamental dependence on God.

Similarly, humility's relation to words like earth, ground, soil, and humus indicates how virtues are cultivated over time and provide a seedbed for the transformation of self and others. One way of referring to virtue is as habituated excellence. Virtues are not outer garments one wears but dispositions that have been shaped and formed in persons over time. Like soil that is fertile for planting, humility is cultivated and nurtured. In soil, the process of decomposition is aided by heat, pressure, and moisture. Small organisms must do their work. Likewise, humility requires time and practice. It demands outside influences and even moments of discomfort or loss, recognitions of our own creatureliness. The earth's humus is created through slow and sometimes invisible changes, and the acquisition of the virtue of humility is no different. Transformation into the image of God is not achieved overnight and certainly not of our own accord. Like soil, we are products of our environment, which is a reminder of the importance of Christian community for learning and inhabiting the particular vision of humility that is described in Philippians 2.

Fertile soil can be incredibly productive. Like the earth's humus, which has exponential value and plays a vital role in its ecosystem, humility has purpose beyond personal formation. Humility is more than an individualized call to Christlikeness. John Wesley emphasized inward *and* outward holiness, or holiness of heart and life, making clear the interconnection of the personal and social. His famous phrase, "The gospel of Christ knows of no religion but social; no holiness but social holiness," asserts that the ultimate purpose of Christian virtue is not personal piety but transformation of the world.[5] In the context of the Christ hymn, humility grounds the hymn's attributes of Christlikeness. Humility functions as an incubating virtue without which other virtues cannot be fostered and Christian witness cannot flourish. Like a seed that sprouted in water or darkness that initially grows fast but cannot sustain life or live

---

5. John Wesley and Charles Wesley, "Preface," *Hymns and Sacred Poems* (London: T. Harris, 1739).

into its fullness, attempting to inhabit Christ's character without humility is no more than a shallow representation of the Christian calling. Christian witness will wither when not grounded by strong, deep roots.

Corporately, then, humility is like the humus of God's reign, a seedbed that nurtures and sustains God's redemptive work in the world. The invitation to be of the same mind as Christ is the primary calling of God's people, which is neither a state of intellectual assent nor a mere act of pietistic pursuit. Having the same mind as Christ entails becoming living embodiments of God's reign. Just as Christ is the *autobasileia* (the kingdom incarnate), God's people are imitators and ambassadors—extensions—of that kingdom.

Humility and Home

Having the same mind as Christ also entails discovering the same rest, assurance, and belonging Jesus finds by being at home with God the Father and God the Spirit. As noted in Romans 8:17, Jesus's heirship is something we are invited to share. Humility is impossible to achieve without locating oneself in relationship with God and others. Again, the etymology of humility reminds us that being placed, like soil and earth, has an essential connection to the virtue of humility. It is no surprise that heroes—who tend to perceive their homes as trivial and confining—struggle with humility.

There are at least two interconnected reasons heroes struggle to embody the virtue of humility. First, the heroic drive often masks an inner insecurity and need for admiration and exaltation. Like Narcissus, heroes can become increasingly infatuated with themselves and fall prey to self-loathing and despair. This dark side of the hero often goes unnoticed, but the underside of most heroic narratives is that the hero needs to be a hero more than the world needs a hero. Maintaining a false or misguided self-image opposes the work of being transformed into the image of God as seen in Christ (Col. 1:15). Heroes need to be elevated, whereas meekness requires recognition of one's lowliness and need for others. The image of God in Christ is not foremost about power or lordship, at least not in the imperial sense, but it is instead about a paradoxical power and lordship that are exemplified through servanthood and sacrifice—the Lamb that was slain.

Second, a hero who is disconnected from home ultimately lacks the necessary bearings for the formation of virtue. Humility is nurtured in the context of the Christian community where the Christian narrative and performances of virtue are exhibited and imparted. But the cultivation of virtue is not a linear process. Only in a loving and mutually affirming community—like that of the Father, Son, and Spirit—can true personhood be discovered. A hero who is disconnected from home faces the exacerbated challenge of the need for admiration coupled with lack of personal identity and worth. As such, the hero's actions are frequently misguided or misdirected. Only after the short-term glory does a longer trajectory of destruction emerge, exposing the deeper story of the hero and their drive for self-worth at the expense of others.

The economy of God's household, represented by the intrapersonal dynamic of Father, Son, and Spirit, helps locate Jesus. Constructive action on behalf of and for the sake of others can only be properly ordered through relationship with God and others. Communities locate human action by providing frameworks through which "good," "right," and "true" are understood. In Jesus we see humility ordered according to its proper ends in God's reign. His humility is not passive or submissive. It is not the abdication of his divinity or a resignation to the powers that be. Christ's humility represents an active confrontation to the temptations of security, glory, and dominance. *Kenosis* (self-emptying) is what Christ chooses in lieu of what the tempter offers in Matthew 4. Jesus can embody humility for the sake of the world because his identity is rooted in relationship with God. He knows his home and there finds peace and assurance—rest—even in the slow and hard work of God's reign.

To walk humbly does not diminish the call to do justice and love mercy. Even in the Christ hymn, justice and mercy coincide with Jesus's embodiment of humility. Similarly, Christians cannot do justice and love kindness (or mercy) aside from the work of embodying Christ's humility. The Christian community remains an interpretive community that helps locate the faithful practice of justice, mercy, and humility in reference to Jesus and God's reign. A hero may claim to be an agent of justice and mercy—and may even appear to be so—but the Christian confession is that embodiment of Christ's humility is constitutive of true justice and mercy.

False and fleeting versions of justice and mercy are common and attractive. Justice and mercy that privilege our own needs for security, power, or preservation, that maintain the normative order, better suit the kingdoms and structures of the world. A triumphal Jesus on a white horse (not a donkey), or who defeats the devil with trickery attends to our own heroic impulses and worldviews. Yet the Way of Jesus is counterintuitive, seemingly even counterproductive. It testifies to a different reign—a different commonwealth—in which the powers and paradigms of the world are called to modesty by the unrelenting love of God. Christians confess what the world does not yet know. The Christ hymn concludes that "at the name of Jesus every knee should bend, . . . and every tongue should confess that Jesus Christ is Lord" (Phil. 2:10b, 11a). This eschatological claim of the recognition of Christ's lordship is not intended to relay a moment when Christians will be justified by their confession, finally having superiority or dominance over an unbelieving world. The claim here is that all will bow, and all will confess. Christ will be known as Lord, and the way of God's reign—*kenosis*—will be recognized as the true order of the world.

✐BE STILL AND KNOW THAT I AM GOD

These chapters have presented the Christian walk as a pilgrimage or journey toward home with God. Home with God is where true belonging and identity are found. There is freedom in the peace and assurance that God is Redeemer and Sustainer and that God's work, not our work, brings salvation to the world. Only here can our aimlessness find direction. Only here can our restlessness find peace. As such, holiness is the pursuit of home with God, a way of life that desires to embody and exhibit the very end it seeks. The journey home is anything but linear, and the meandering pilgrim must learn to faithfully dance, to engage the choreography of the quotidian in ways that reflect Christ's likeness to the world.

Psalm 46 has been an important psalm for God's people throughout the centuries. It speaks of God as "our refuge and strength" and our "help in trouble" (v. 1). Amid uncertainty and pending calamity, Psalm 46 is a reminder that God is sovereign and will ultimately prevail. Many Protestant Christians know

Martin Luther's hymn "A Mighty Fortress Is our God," which is based on Psalm 46. The first line of Psalm 46:10 is even more widely known and cited: "Be still, and know that I am God!" In many ways, this book is about learning how to be still and seeking to know God.

To be still and know may sound like a command to disengage or to be passive. It could be read as a call to inaction or to withdraw to a place of shelter while God engages external forces. To be still and know God, however, is a form of proactive witness in a restless world. God calls God's people to testify to a new reality in which the fears and motivations that drive our disconnectedness, impulsiveness, and heroism are confronted by the deep peace and assurance that come from finding rest in God.

In this regard, to be still and know God reveals the paradox of the Christian journey: to be still yet on the move, ever professing Christ's lordship; to know God yet ever seeking deeper understanding of God and remaining curious about each small revelation along life's path. The great threat to being still and knowing God is the assumption that we have arrived or already have full knowledge. That arrogance quickly leads to idolatry, turning stillness into complacency and knowledge into a weapon. Instead, holiness is about the pursuit itself, which makes stillness and knowledge possible. If God is for us, then we need not worry who is against us (Rom. 8:31); we need not rely on our own strength and laurels; we need not coerce, control, or scheme. Pursuit of home with God arises from the deep awareness that our hearts are restless until they find rest in God and that, along the journey, God is with us.

✒ACKNOWLEDGMENTS

Many people have played a role in bringing this book to fruition. Good work is a collective enterprise, and this book is undoubtedly better because of the feedback and support offered by colleagues and friends.

We are grateful for the invitation from Mount Vernon Nazarene University to provide the Hicks Holiness Lectures in the spring of 2019. Those lectures, and subsequent conversations with faculty and students, prompted this book's topic and structure.

We are thankful for the encouragement of the Nazarene Compassionate Ministries global team and Josh's spring 2021 sabbatical from Nazarene Theological Seminary. Such support is a gift.

A special thanks to Bonnie Perry for her encouragement of this project, to Dean Blevins for his review and feedback on an early manuscript, and to Audra Spiven for her skillful editorial work and management of this publication.

Joshua R. Sweeden
Nell M. Becker Sweeden